1 a Work out

    i $2^3 \times 2^3$ ....

    ii 2^6 ....

    iii What do you notice? ....

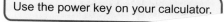

Use the power key on your calculator.

b Work out

    i $2^5 \times 2^2$ ....

    ii 2^7 ....

    iii What do you notice? ....

G000116071

c Complete the multiplication table of powers of 5. Write your answers as powers of 5.

×	5^3	5^4	5^5
5^2			
5^3			
5^4			

 Guided

2 Write each product as a single power.

    a $3^2 \times 3^5 \times 3^3 = 3^{\cdots + \cdots + \cdots} = 3^{\cdots}$

    b $4^3 \times 4^4 \times 4$ ....

4 can be written as 4^1 (4 to the power 1).

Worked example

3 Write these calculations using powers of the same number. Give your answers in index form.

    a 16×2^3 ....

    b 27×3^2 ....

    c $27 \times 9 \times 3$ ....

$16 = 2 \times 2 \times 2 \times 2 = 2^4$

$27 = 3 \times 3 \times 3$

Index is the name for the small raised number in a power. Indices is the plural of index.

 Guided

4 Write each division as a single power.

    a $2^7 \div 2^4 = 2^{\cdots - \cdots} = 2^{\cdots}$

    b $5^7 \div 5^3$ ....

You can subtract the indices only when dividing powers of the same number.

5 Work out these. Check your answers using a calculator.

    a $[3 \times (2 + 2)]^2 = [3 \times 4]^2 = 12^2 =$ ....

    b $[(9 + 9) \div 6]^2 = [18 \div 6]^2 = \ldots^2 = \ldots$

    c $[64 \div (10 - 8)^3 + 2] \div 5$ ....

Work out the inner brackets first. $(2 + 2) = 4$

Guided

Literacy hint

Square brackets [ ] make the inner and outer brackets easier to see. Input them as round brackets on your calculator.

6 Work out

$(-2)^2 = -2 \times -2$

    a $5 + (-2)^2$ ....
    b $-5 - 2^2$ ....

    c $(-4)^2 - 4$ ....
    d $4 - (-3)^2$ ....

 Guided

7 Write each of these using a single power.

    a $(-2)^3 \times (-2)^4 = (-2)^{\cdots + \cdots} =$ ....
    b $(-6)^6 \times (-6)^3$ ....

    c $(-3)^5 \div (-3)^3 = (-3)^{\cdots - \cdots} =$ ....
    d $(-8)^5 \div (-8)^2$ ....

CHECK Tick each box as your **confidence** in this topic improves.

Need extra help? Go to page 5 and tick the boxes next to Q1, 2 and 4–7. Then have a go at them once you've finished 1.1–1.4.

1 Work out

a $\sqrt[3]{27}$ ....

b $\sqrt[3]{64}$ ....

c $\sqrt[3]{-27}$ ....

$\boxed{\square \times \square \times \square = -27}$

d $\sqrt[3]{-64}$ ....

2 Problem-solving A metal cube has a volume of 1000 cm³.

a Work out the side length of the cube. $\sqrt[3]{1000}$ = ... cm

b Work out the surface area of the cube. ....

c The cube is melted down and made into eight identical cubes. Work out the surface area of one of these cubes.

$1000 \div 8 =$ .... cm³, so side length = ...

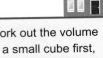

Work out the volume of a small cube first, and then work out the side length.

3 $c = \sqrt{b^2 - a^2}$

Find the value of c when

a $a = 3$ and $b = 5$ ....

b $a = 5$ and $b = 6$ correct to 1 decimal place. ....

4 Modelling / Reasoning The length L cm of the shell of a type of sea turtle can be estimated from its mass m kg using the formula $L = \sqrt[3]{5000m}$.

a Estimate the shell length of a turtle with a mass of 40 kg. Give your answer correct to 2 decimal places.

b Govinda says that the most accurate way to write the answer to part **a** is $\sqrt[3]{200\,000}$. Is she correct? Explain your answer.

5 a Estimate the answers to these.

i $(218 - 21.4) \div (35.4 + 7.1)$ $200 \div$ .... = ...

ii $16.4 \div (9.6 - \sqrt[3]{9.3})$ ....

$218 - 21.4$ is approximately 200.
$35.4 + 7.1$ is approximately $\square$.

When approximating $\sqrt[3]{9.3}$, choose the closest cube number.

b Use a calculator to work out each answer. Give your answers correct to 1 decimal place.

i ....   **ii** ....

6 Work out

a $\dfrac{5^2 \times 4^2}{2^2} = \dfrac{5 \times 5 \times 4 \times 4}{2 \times 2} = \dfrac{5 \times 5 \times \overset{2}{\cancel{4}} \times \overset{2}{\cancel{4}}}{\cancel{2}^1 \times \cancel{2}^1} = 5 \times 5 \times$ .... $\times$ .... = ...

$\boxed{\text{Cancel the common factors.}}$

b $\dfrac{(8 \times 3)^2}{4^2} = \dfrac{8^2 \times 3^2}{4^2}$

$\boxed{(8 \times 3)^2 = (8 \times 3) \times (8 \times 3) = 8^2 \times 3^2}$

7 Work out $\dfrac{18 \times 100}{(3 \times 5)^2}$

Need extra help? Go to page 6 and tick the boxes next to Q8 and 9. Then have a go at them once you've finished 1.1–1.4.

1 Complete the table of prefixes.

Prefix	Letter	Power	Number
tera	T		1 000 000 000 000
giga	G	10^9	1 000 000 000
mega	M		1 000 000
kilo	k	10^3	
deci	d	10^{-1}	0.1

Prefix	Letter	Power	Number
centi	c	10^{-2}	
milli	m		0.001
micro	μ	10^{-6}	
nano	n		0.000 000 001
pico	p	10^{-12}	

> Some powers of 10 have a name called a prefix. Each prefix is represented by a letter.
> For example, mega means 10^6 and is represented by the letter M, as in MW for megawatt.

Literacy hint

μ, the letter for the prefix micro, is the Greek letter mu.

2 Work out these conversions.

a 1 megabyte (MB) to B .... B

b 1 kilometre (km) to m .... m

c 1 milligram (mg) to g .... g

d 1 nanometre (nm) to m .... m

3 How many milliseconds are in a second? ....

4 a Write as a fraction.

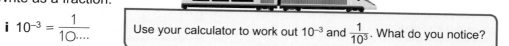

i $10^{-3} = \dfrac{1}{10^{....}}$

Use your calculator to work out 10^{-3} and $\dfrac{1}{10^3}$. What do you notice?

ii $10^{-5} = \dfrac{1}{10^{....}}$

b Complete the rule: $10^{-x} = \dfrac{1}{10^{....}}$

Worked example

Literacy hint

A transistor is the basic building block of all modern electronic devices.

5 STEM A full stop on this page is approximately 0.5 mm wide. The world's smallest transistor is 1 μm wide.

How many transistors can fit across a full stop?

Strategy hint

Convert both measurements to the same units first.

6 a Complete the sequence. Write your answers as whole numbers or fractions.

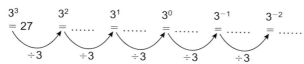

3^3 3^2 3^1 3^0 3^{-1} 3^{-2}
= 27 = ... = ... = ... = ... = ...

÷3 ÷3 ÷3 ÷3 ÷3

b Use your calculator to work out 3^0. ......

c Use your calculator to work out 4^0. ......

d What do you notice? ....

e What is 12^0? ......

7 Work out these. Write each answer as a whole number or a fraction.

a $2^3 \div 2^5$ ....

b $2^5 \div 2^5$ ....

c $1 \div 2^{-2}$ ....

d $\dfrac{2^4 \times 2^3}{2^5}$ ....

CHECK Tick each box as your **confidence** in this topic improves.

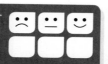

Need extra help? Go to page 5 and tick the boxes next to Q3, 4 and 5. Then have a go at them once you've finished 1.1–1.4.

1 Work out

   a 5×10^2 ....

   b 2.5×10^4 ....

   c 4×10^{-2} ....

   d 2.9×10^{-5} ....

> Multiplying by a negative power of 10 is the same as dividing by a positive power of 10. For example,
> $3 \times 10^{-4} = 3 \times \dfrac{1}{10^4} = 3 \div 10^4$
> $= 3 \div 10\,000 = 0.0003$

2 Reasoning

   a **i** Write $5^2 \times 5^2 \times 5^2$ as a single power. ....

      ii Complete: $5^2 \times 5^2 \times 5^2 = (5^2)^{\cdots}$

   b **i** Write $6^3 \times 6^3 \times 6^3 \times 6^3 \times 6^3$ as a single power. ....

      ii Complete: $6^3 \times 6^3 \times 6^3 \times 6^3 \times 6^3 = (6^3)^{\cdots}$

   c Use your answers to parts **a** and **b** to complete the rule: $(p^a)^b = p^{\cdots}$

3 Using algebra, standard form is $A \times 10^n$ where $1 \leqslant A < 10$ and n is an integer.

   Circle the numbers written in standard form.

   A 6.8×10^3 B 9.995×10^8 C 10×10^{-2}

   D 5.5×10^{-5} E 1.5 billion

> A number written in standard form is a number between 1 and 10 multiplied by 10 to a power. For example, 3.5×10^5 is written in standard form because 3.5 lies between 1 and 10. 35×10^5 is not in standard form because 35 does not lie between 1 and 10.

4 Write each number using standard form.

Guided

   a $6000 = 6\,\overset{\frown}{0}\,\overset{\frown}{0}\,\overset{\frown}{0} = 6 \times 10^{\cdots}$

   b $7\,500\,000$ ....

   c $0.000\,07 = 0.\overset{\frown}{0}\overset{\frown}{0}\overset{\frown}{0}\overset{\frown}{0}7 = 7 \times 10^{-\cdots}$

   d 0.8 ....

> 6 lies between 1 and 10. Multiply by the power of 10 needed to give the original number.

5 STEM Write each quantity using standard form.

   a Alpha Centauri is the nearest binary star system to our solar system. It is $41\,000\,000\,000\,000\,000$ m from Earth.

   b One atom of gold has a mass of $0.000\,000\,000\,000\,000\,000\,000\,33$ g.

> **Literacy hint**
> A binary star is a star system consisting of two stars orbiting around each other.

6 STEM / Reasoning 'Avogadro's number' is a very important number in chemistry. It is 6.02×10^{23}.

   a Is the number 6.02×10^{23} written using standard form? ....

   b Write this as an ordinary number.

   c Enter the number into your calculator and press the = key.

      Compare your calculator display with the standard form number.

      Explain how your calculator displays a number in standard form.

 CHECK Tick each box as your **confidence** in this topic improves.

> **Need extra help?** Go to page 6 and tick the boxes next to Q10–14. Then have a go at them once you've finished 1.1–1.4.

1 Strengthen

Indices and powers of 10

1 Write each product as a single power.

a $5^2 \times 5^4 = 5 \cdots + \cdots = 5 \cdots$

b $8^3 \times 8^4 = 8^{3 \cdots 4} = 8 \cdots$

c $10^4 \times 10$ ....

d $2^3 \times 2^4 \times 2^2$ ....

How many 5s are multiplied together?

$$5^2 \times 5^4 = \underbrace{5 \times 5}_{2} \times \underbrace{5 \times 5 \times 5 \times 5}_{4}$$

Write 10 as the power 10^1.

2 Write each division as a single power.

a $3^6 \div 3^4 = 3 \cdots - \cdots = 3 \cdots$

b $9^5 \div 9^2 = 9^{5 \cdots 2} = 9 \cdots$

c $4^8 \div 4^2$ ....

d $2^4 \div 2$ ....

How many 3s are left after cancelling four of them?

$$3^6 \div 3^4 = \frac{3^6}{3^4} = \frac{\overbrace{\cancel{3} \times \cancel{3} \times \cancel{3} \times \cancel{3} \times 3 \times 3}^{6}}{\underbrace{\cancel{3} \times \cancel{3} \times \cancel{3} \times \cancel{3}}_{4}}$$

3 Convert the units.

a 0.63 km to m ....

b 0.708 m to μm ....

c 8200 nm to m ....

d 53 000 mm to km ....

Multiply to convert bigger units to smaller units.
Divide to convert smaller units to bigger units.

4 a i Complete the following: $3^2 \div 3^2 = \dfrac{3^2}{3^2} = \dfrac{\cdots}{\cdots} = \cdots$

ii Complete the following: $3^2 \div 3^2 = 3^{\cdots - \cdots} = 3 \cdots$

iii What is the value of 3^0? .....

b i Work out $3^3 \div 3^5$.

ii Use your answer to part **b i** to complete: $3^{-\cdots} = \dfrac{1}{3^{\cdots}}$

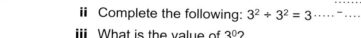

$$3^3 \div 3^5 = \frac{3^3}{3^5} = \frac{\cancel{3} \times \cancel{3} \times \cancel{3}}{\cancel{3} \times \cancel{3} \times \cancel{3} \times 3 \times 3} = \frac{1}{3 \times 3} = \frac{1}{3^{\square}} = 3^{-\square}$$

5 Write each of these as a single power.

a $2^5 \times 2^{-2} = 2^{5 + -2} = 2 \cdots$

b $5^{-2} \times 5^{-5} = 5^{\cdots + \cdots} = 5 \cdots$

c $3^3 \div 3^8 = 3^{\cdots - \cdots} = 3 \cdots$

d $\dfrac{7^3}{7^6} = 7^3 \div 7^6 =$ ....

e $10^2 \times 10^{-4} \times 10^{-3}$ ....

f $10^{-4} \div 10^{-7} \times 10^2$ ....

6 a Write 27 as a power of 3. ....

$27 = 3 \times 3 \times \square$. How many 3s are multiplied together to make 27?

b Use your answer to write each product as a single power of 3.

i 27×3^2 ....

ii $3^5 \times 27$ ....

iii 27×27 ....

Powers and roots

7 Work out

Use the priority of operations to help you.
Calculate the inside brackets first.

a $[20 - (15 - 4)] = [20 - \cdots] = \cdots$

b $[20 - (15 - 4)]^2$ ....

Use your answer to part **a**.

c $[(7 + 5) \div 3]^2$ ....

d $(3 \times 3 + 2)^2$ ....

8 Reasoning a Use the x^2 key of your calculator to work out

    i -5^2 ....

    ii $(-5)^2$ ....

  b Explain why you get two different answers.

  c Use your answers to work out

    i $50 + (-5)^2$ ....

    ii $50 - 5^2$ ....

    iii $-4^2 - (-2)^2$ ....

9 a Jonti estimates $\frac{24.5}{8.1} + 7.7$ as $\frac{24}{8} + 8 = 3 + 8 = 11$.

    Why did he round 24.5 down and not up?

> Was the reason that 8.1 was rounded down so it's more accurate to round the numerator down too, or was it that $24 \div 8$ is easier than $25 \div 8$, or was it both reasons?

  b Estimate $\frac{19.1}{3.6} - 3.5$

Standard form

10 STEM The Pierre Guillaumat supertanker was the heaviest ship ever built, at 2.7×10^8 kg.
Write this as an ordinary number.

11 Work out

  a 5.2×10^{-2} ....

  b 7.6×10^{-6} ....

> $5 \cdot 2 \\ 0 \cdot 0 5 2$ $\times 10^{-2}$ means $\div 10^2$, so divide by 10 two times.

12 Write each number using standard form.

> A number written using standard form looks like this.
>
> $$A \times 10^n$$
>
> number between 1 and 10   times sign   power of 10

  a $8200 = 8\,2\,0\,0 = 8.2 \times 10\cdots$

  b $720\,000$ ....

13 Write each number using standard form.

  a $0.000\,35 = 0.0\,0\,0\,3\,5 = 3.5 \times 10\cdots$

  b $0.000\,002\,8$ ....

14 Write this set of standard form numbers in order, from smallest to largest.

    9.9×10^3 5.5×10^6 6.6×10^{-5} 1.1×10^{-2}

1 Reasoning a Work out

    i $(-1)^2$ ....   **ii** $(-1)^3$ ....   **iii** $(-1)^4$ ....   **iv** $(-1)^5$ ....

  b **i** What do you notice about the signs of the answers?

    ii Write a rule that gives the sign of a power of a negative number.

  c Test that your rule works for another negative number and powers.

  d Does the rule work for negative indices?

2 Reasoning Rewrite each calculation with brackets so that it gives the target number. If necessary, use square brackets for outer brackets.

  a $10 \times 2 + 4^2$ Target 360 ....

  b $9 - 4 - 2^2$ Target 49 ....

  c $5\sqrt{64} - \sqrt{16}$ Target 20 ....

3 Problem-solving Some 18 cm by 24 cm tiles are used to cover the floor of a kitchen measuring 5 m by 3 m. Find the best way to estimate the number of tiles. State whether your answer is an overestimate or an underestimate.

> **Strategy hint**
>
> Make some sketches. Why is your way the best?

4 Problem-solving / Finance

  a A mountain bike priced at £595 was sold in a sale at 37.5% off. Estimate the sale price.

  b Some experts say that the world's total of mined gold would fit into a cube with a volume of 8870 m³. Estimate the length of one side of the cube.

5 STEM The coordinates of the centre of a circle are (4, 7) and the coordinates of a point on the circle are (12.1, 10.7). This formula gives the radius r of the circle.

$$r = \sqrt{(12.1 - 4)^2 + (10.7 - 7)^2}$$

Estimate r.

6 Write these quantities using an appropriate prefix.

a 4.8×10^{-3} m ....

b 2.5×10^6 t ....

c 3×10^{12} W ....

d 1.25×10^{-6} g ....

7 Write each of these as a simplified product of powers.

a $10^3 \times 2^4 \times 5^2$ ....

$10^3 = (2 \times 5)^3$

b $20^2 \times 2^4 \times 5^3$ ....

8 Solve the equation $4x^6 \times x^{-4} = 36$.

9 Here are some incorrect answers given by students when asked to write numbers in standard form. Rewrite each answer correctly.

Worked example

a 36×10^4 ....

b 0.225×10^6 ....

c 169×10^{-3} ....

d 0.016×10^{-10} ....

10 Write these as a single power of the smallest possible integer.

a $(5^4)^{11}$ ....

b $[(7^2)^3]^4$ ....

c 1000^{20} ....

11 Write these numbers using standard form.

a 8 hundred ....

b 19 hundredths ....

c 14 thousand ....

d 147 thousandths ....

e 0.25 million ....

f 72 billionths ....

thousandths = $\times 10^{-3}$, millionths = $\times 10^{-6}$, billionths = $\times 10^{-9}$.

Watch out! $0.25 \times 10^{\square}$ is not in standard form.

12 STEM The distance of Neptune from Earth is approximately 4.5×10^9 km.

Light travels at approximately 300 000 000 m/s.

Use the formula time = $\dfrac{\text{distance}}{\text{speed}}$ to estimate the time taken for light to travel from Neptune to Earth. Give your answer in minutes.

PROGRESS BAR Colour in the progress bar as you get questions correct.
Then fill in the progression chart on pages 104–108.

1 Write each calculation as a power of a single number.

a $10^2 \times 10^6$ ....

b $5^3 \times 5^4$ ....

c 8×8^5 ....

2 Six square panes of glass are used to make a glass cube with volume $27\,m^3$.
Work out the area of each square pane.

3 Write each calculation as a single power.

a $3^5 \times 3^2 \div 3^4$ ....

b 16×2^3 ....

4 Work out $10^0 - 5^0$ ....

5 Work out $10^2 - (-5)^2$ ....

6 Work out a good estimate for each calculation.

a 11.6×1.7 ....

b $4.3 \times \sqrt{27}$ ....

7 **Real** A pack of laminate flooring covers $2.22\,m^2$. Liam wants to cover a floor area of $23.5\,m^2$.

He needs to estimate the calculation $\frac{23.5}{2.22}$ to find the number of packs to buy.

Which of these estimates gives the closest answer: $\frac{24}{2}$, $\frac{25}{2}$ or $\frac{25}{2.5}$? Explain why.

What will happen if Liam uses this estimate?

8 A power station can generate $8.2\,GW$ (gigawatts) of power.

a How many watts is this? ....

b How many MW (megawatts) is this? ....

9 Write each of these as an ordinary number.

a 5.1×10^6 ....

b 9×10^{-5} ....

10 Work out

a $\left(\frac{10}{5}\right)^2$ ....

b $\frac{(4 \times 5)^2}{2^2 \times 2^3}$ ....

11 The concrete used to build the Hoover Dam in the USA has a mass of $5\,300\,000$ tonnes.
Write this mass

a using a suitable prefix ....

b using standard form. ....

12 Write each number using standard form.

a $0.000\,000\,000\,082$ ....

b 240 million ....

2.1 Substituting into expressions

1 Write down the missing lengths.

a
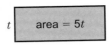
t | area = $5t$

....

b

t | area = t^2

....

c
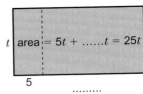
t | area = $5t +$ ......$t = 25t$

5

....

2 Work out the area of each shape in Question 1 when $t = 4$.

a

b

c

 Guided

3 Work out the value of these expressions when $x = 2$ and $y = 3$.

a $5x + y^2 = 5 \times 2 + 3 \times 3 =$ .... $+$ .... $=$ ....

b $5y^2 = 5 \times 3 \times 3 =$ ....

c $3x^3$

d $10y^3 - 10x$

e $(3x + 2y)^2 = (3 \times 2 + 2 \times 3)^2 = ($......$ + $......$)^2 = ($......$)^2 =$ ....

f $xy + (7x - 4y)^3$

> Substitute the values of x and y.

> Work out the brackets first, then work out the index (power).

4 Work out the value of these expressions when $p = 3$, $q = 4$ and $r = 5$.

a $2p^2q$

b $100 - (p^3 - r)$

c $\dfrac{pq + pr}{q + r}$

> $\dfrac{pq + pr}{q + r}$ is the same as $(pq + pr) \div (q + r)$

5 Work out the value of each expression when $a = 2$, $b = 3$ and $c = -4$.

a $3a(a + c)$

b $5a^2(ab + bc)$

c $\sqrt{3 + ab}$

d $\sqrt[3]{9b} + c^2$

6 Using the values of the letters in the table, ring the correct answer for each of these.

Letter	p	q	r	s	t
Value	18	9	6	−1	−3

a $p + (qs)^2$ A −63   B 82   C 99

b $(r + t)^3 - 3q$ A −54   B 0   C 702

c $r\sqrt{q} - 5st$ A 3   B 33   C 39

d $\sqrt[3]{p + q} - r^2$ A −33   B 9   C 39

CHECK Tick each box as your **confidence** in this topic improves.

Need extra help? Go to page 15 and tick the boxes next to Q2, 3 and 4. Then have a go at them once you've finished 2.1–2.5.

2.2 Writing expressions and formulae

1 A waiter's daily pay is worked out using the number of hours worked, w, the hourly rate of pay, h, the total amount in tips, e, and the number of staff who share the tip, n.

a Work out how much a waiter is paid for working a 6-hour day at an hourly rate of £6.50. The total of £105 tips is shared between 5 staff.

$$6 \times \text{........} + \frac{105}{5} = \text{..........} + \text{..........} = \text{..........}$$

> A formula is a rule that shows a relationship between two or more variables (letters). You can use substitution to find each unknown value.

b Write an expression for the daily pay in terms of w, h, e and n.

$$wh + \frac{\text{.......}}{\text{......}}$$

c Write a formula for the daily pay, P, in terms of w, h, e and n.

> This formula has '$P =$' in front of the expression from part **b**.

d Use your formula to work out P when $w = 5$, $h = £7$, $e = £350$ and $n = 10$.

2 Real / Modelling To roast a turkey takes 15 minutes per $\frac{1}{2}$ kg plus an extra 60 minutes.

a How long does it take to roast a turkey that weighs 5 kg?

> How much time for every kilogram?

b Write an expression for the number of minutes it takes to cook a turkey that weighs x kg.

c Write a formula to work out the number of minutes, M, it takes to cook a turkey that weighs x kg.

d Use your formula to work out M when $x = 4.2$.

e What time should you put a 4 kg turkey in the oven to be ready at 2 pm?

3 Real / Problem-solving The graph shows the amount it costs to hire a private jet.

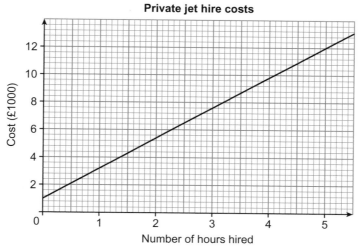

Private jet hire costs

Write a formula for the total cost, C, to hire a private jet for h hours.

CHECK Tick each box as your **confidence** in this topic improves.

Need extra help? Go to page 15 and tick the box next to Q6. Then have a go at it once you've finished 2.1–2.5.

2.3 STEM: Using formulae

1 STEM You can use this formula to work out the pressure acting on a surface.

$$P = \frac{F}{A}$$

where

P = pressure (newtons per square metre, N/m²), F = force (newtons, N), A = area (square metres, m²).

Work out the value of the pressure when

a $F = 200$ and $A = 2$

b $F = 3000$ and $A = 0.5$

2 STEM / Modelling You can use this formula to work out the kinetic energy of a moving object.

$$E = \frac{1}{2}mv^2$$

where

E = kinetic energy (joules, J), m = mass (kg), v = velocity (metres/second, m/s).

Work out the kinetic energy E when

a $m = 50$ and $v = 3$

b $m = 0.2$ and $v = 100$

> **Literacy hint**
>
> The kinetic energy of an object is the energy it possesses due to its motion.

3 STEM Use the formula $v = u + at$ to work out the value of

a t when $v = 35$, $u = 20$ and $a = 5$

b a when $v = 42$, $u = 10$ and $t = 8$

Guided

$v = u + at$

$35 = 20 + 5t$

$35 - 20 = 5t$

$15 = 5t$

$t = \dots\dots$

> Substitute the numbers that you know into the formula. Solve the equation, one step at a time, to find the value of t.

4 Make the letter in brackets the subject of each formula.

Guided

a $A = bh$ (b)

$b \longrightarrow \boxed{\times h} \longrightarrow A$

$\dfrac{A}{h} \longleftarrow \boxed{\div h} \longleftarrow A$

$b = \dots\dots\dots$

> You change the subject of a formula by rearranging the formula to get the letter that you want on its own on one side of the equation. Rearrange the formula $A = bh$ so it starts '$b =$'.

> The subject of a formula is always the letter on its own on one side of the equation. For example, the subject of $E = \frac{1}{2}mv^2$ is E.

b $s = xy$ (x)

c $t = p + 5y$ (p)

d $u = \dfrac{t}{10}$ (t)

e $v = \dfrac{y}{x}$ (x)

> **Worked example**
>
>

CHECK Tick each box as your confidence in this topic improves.

Need extra help? Go to pages 15 and 16 tick the boxes next to Q5 and 7. Then have a go at them once you've finished 2.1–2.5.

2.4 Rules of indices and brackets

1 Expand these brackets.

a $t(t^2 - 2t + 3) = t \times t^2 - t \times 2t + t \times 3 =$ .... − .... + ...

b $2a(2a^2 + 3a + 4)$ ....

c $x^2(5x^2 - 4x - 3)$ ....

> When you expand brackets, you multiply every term inside the brackets by the term outside the brackets.

Worked example

2 Expand and simplify.

a $p(p^2 + 5p) + 5p(p^2 + 2p)$

> Expand both brackets separately, then simplify by collecting like terms.

b $5r(3 + 4r + 5r^2) - 2r(10r^2 + 5r - 3)$

3 Problem-solving / Reasoning Show that $n(3n^2 + 4n) + 2n^3 = 4n^2(4n + 1) - 11n^3$.

> **Strategy hint**
> Expand and simplify each side of the equation separately, and then show that both expressions are the same.

4 Simplify these terms.

a $(3a)^2 = 3a \times 3a =$ ....

b $(2x)^3$ ....

c $\left(\dfrac{c}{2}\right)^3 = \dfrac{c^3}{2^3} = \dfrac{c^3}{\text{.......}}$

d $\left(\dfrac{a}{5}\right)^2$ ....

5 Write true (T) or false (F) for each of these.

a $10^0 = 10$ ....

b $5^0 = 1$ ....

c $h^0 = 0$ ....

d $5f^0 = 5$ ....

> Any number or letter to the power zero = 1.
> In part **d**, $5f^0 = 5 \times f^0$

6 Simplify these expressions. Write each one as a negative power and as a fraction.

a $\dfrac{x^5}{x^8} = x^{5-8} = x^{\cdots} = \dfrac{1}{x^{\cdots}}$

> Any whole number or letter to a negative power can be written as a fraction with a numerator of 1, e.g. $p^{-2} = \dfrac{1}{p^2}$

b $\dfrac{a}{a^6}$ ....

c $h^4 \div h^{10}$ ....

7 Factorise each expression completely. Check your answer.

> To factorise an expression completely, take out the highest common factor (HCF) of its terms.

a $8x + 4 = 4(\text{.......}x + \text{.......})$

Check: $4(\text{.......}x + \text{.......}) = 4 \times \text{.......}x + 4 \times \text{.......} = 8x + 4$ ✓

b $5x^3 - 10x^2 = \text{.......}x^{\cdots}(\text{.......} - \text{.......})$

> The HCF of $5x^3$ and $10x^2$ is $5x^2$.
> $5x^2 \times x = 5x^3$ and $5x^2 \times 2 = 10x^2$

Check: $\text{.......}x^{\cdots}(\text{.......} - \text{.......}) = $ ....

c $12x^6 + 4x^3$

8 Factorise each expression completely. Check your answer.

a $5a + 10b + 15c$

> The HCF of $5a$, $10b$ and $15c$ is 5.

b $2x^2 + 4x^3 - 6xy$

> What is the HCF of $2x^2$, $4x^3$ and $6xy$?

CHECK Tick each box as your **confidence** in this topic improves.

Need extra help? Go to pages 15 and 16 tick the boxes next to Q1, 8, 9, 10 and 11. Then have a go at them once you've finished 2.1–2.5.

2.5 Expanding double brackets

1 Work out an expression for the area of the rectangle.

Write the expression in its simplest form.

Guided

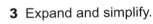

$(x + 2)(x + 6) = x^2 + 6x + \text{.........} + \text{.........}$

$= \text{.................................}$

> When you expand double brackets, you multiply each term in one bracket by each term in the other bracket.
> $(a + b)(c + d) = ac + ad + bc + bd$

> **Worked example**
>

2 Problem-solving / Reasoning Work out an expression for the area of this rectangle.

3 Expand and simplify.

Guided

a $(p + 3)(p + 4) = p \times p + p \times 4 + 3 \times p + 3 \times 4$ **b** $(r + 4)(r + 5)$

$= \text{.................................}$

$= \text{.............................}$

c $(y + 3)(y - 4)$ **d** $(x - 5)(x - 2)$

> In part **c**, watch out for the minus sign.
> In part **d**, $-5 \times -2 = +10$

4 Problem-solving / Reasoning Millie and Phoebe both expand and simplify the quadratic expression $(h - 5)(3 + h)$.

Millie says that the answer is $h^2 + 2h - 15$.

Phoebe says that the answer is $h^2 - 2h - 15$.

Only one of them is correct. Who is it? What mistake was made?

> A quadratic expression is one that contains a squared term and no higher powers.

5 Complete these expansions. Simplify each answer.

a $(x + 2)(x - 6) + x(3x - 4)$

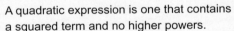

> Work out $(x + 2)(x - 6)$.
> Expand $x(3x - 4)$.
> Add them together.

b $(a - 3)(a - 5) - 6(a - 4)$

6 Problem-solving / Reasoning Show that $x(x + 5) - 3(x + 4) = (x + 4)(x - 4) + 2(x + 2)$.

CHECK Tick each box as your **confidence** in this topic improves.

Need extra help? Go to page 16 and tick the box next to Q12. Then have a go at it once you've finished 2.1–2.5.

2 Strengthen

Substituting into expressions

1 Use the priority of operations to write these in order of size, smallest first.

> Brackets before powers.

$5(14 - 6)$ $(3 \times 4 - 10 \div 2)^2$ $16 + \dfrac{4^3}{2}$ $5^2 + 2 \times 10$

Guided

2 Work out the value of the following expressions when $p = 5$ and $q = 2$.

   a $4p^2 = 4 \times p \times p = 4 \times$ .... $\times$ .... $=$ ....

   b $(2p)^3 = (2 \times p)^3 = (2 \times$ ....$)^3 =$ .... $\times$ .... $\times$ .... $=$ ....

   c $\dfrac{9p + q^2}{p + q} = \dfrac{9 \times 5 + 2 \times 2}{..... + ...} = \dfrac{....... + ...}{.......} = \dfrac{.......}{.......} = $ ......

   d $10(p^2 - q^2)$

3 Work out

   a $6 + -2$ ....

   b $-10 - -8$ ....

   c -5×3 ....

   d $(-2)^2$ ....

Check your answers with a calculator.

> $(-2)^2 = -2 \times -2 = \square$

Guided

4 Find the value of each expression when $p = -2$, $q = 4$ and $r = 5$.

   a $2r + p = 2 \times$ .... $+$ .... $=$ .... $-$ .... $=$ ....

   b $q^2 - p =$ ....$^2 -$ .... $=$ .... $+$ .... $=$ ....

   c $2q^2 - pr$ ....

   d $\dfrac{q - p}{2r}$ ....

   e $p^3 + 2r$ ....

> **Worked example**
>
>

Writing and using formulae

5 Use the formula $P = Hn$ to work out the value of P when

   a $H = 5$ and $n = 7$

   b $H = 4.4$ and $n = 0.5$

6 A canoe shop charges an amount per hour to hire a canoe.
It also charges a one-off cost to hire safety equipment.

Guided

   a Work out the total cost to hire a canoe for 2 hours at £15 per hour
when the one-off safety equipment cost is £20.

      $2 \times$ .... $+$ .... $=$ ....

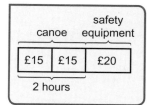

   b Write an expression for the total cost to hire a canoe for c hours
at £h per hour when the one-off safety equipment cost is £s.

      .... $\times$ .... $+$ .... $=$ .... $+$ ....

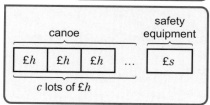

   c Write a formula for the total cost, T, in terms of c, h and s. ....

   d Use your formula to work out T when $c = 6$, $h = 5$ and $s = 8$. ....

7 STEM You can use this formula to calculate the volume of a certain shape of pyramid.

$V = \dfrac{s^2 h}{2c}$

Work out the value of V when $s = 2$, $h = 12$ and $c = 3$.

$V = \dfrac{2^2 \times 12}{2 \times 3} = \dfrac{\square \times 12}{\square} = \dfrac{\square}{\square} = \square$

Expanding, factorising and indices

8 Use a grid method to expand

a $t(t^2 - 2t + 9)$

b $2a(3a^2 + 5a + 11)$

You can use a grid method to expand brackets like this.
$d(d^2 + 5d - 2)$

×	d^2	$+5d$	-2
d	d^3	$+5d^2$	$-2d$

Answer: $d^3 + 5d^2 - 2d$

9 Simplify

a $(2t)^3 = 2t \times 2t \times 2t = 2 \times 2 \times 2 \times t \times t \times t = \underline{\hspace{1cm}} t^3$

b $(5a)^2$ ....

c $\left(\dfrac{b}{4}\right)^2 = \dfrac{b}{4} \times \dfrac{b}{4} = \dfrac{b \times b}{4 \times 4} = \dfrac{b^2}{\underline{\hspace{0.5cm}}}$

d $\left(\dfrac{x}{2}\right)^3$ ....

10 Complete these.

a $5^{-2} = \dfrac{1}{5^{\cdots}}$

b $5^{-4} = \dfrac{1}{5^{\cdots}}$

c $a^{-2} = \dfrac{1}{a^{\cdots}}$

$5^{-3} = \dfrac{1}{5^3}$

11 a What is the highest common factor of

  i $4x$ and 12 ....

  ii $3y^2$ and $6y^3$? ....

The HCF of 3 and 6 is 3. y^2 is also a common factor.

  b Factorise each expression completely by taking out the highest common factor.

  i $4x - 12 = \underline{\hspace{0.5cm}}(\underline{\hspace{0.5cm}} - \underline{\hspace{0.5cm}})$

Check your answer by expanding the bracket.

  ii $6y^3 + 3y^2$ ....

  iii $6a + 8b + 12c = \underline{\hspace{0.5cm}}(\underline{\hspace{0.5cm}} + \underline{\hspace{0.5cm}} + \underline{\hspace{0.5cm}})$

What is the HCF of $6a$, $8b$ and $12c$?

  iv $5p^2 + 10pq - 20px$ ....

Worked example

12 Expand and simplify

a $(x + 5)(x + 3)$

b $(x + 5)(x - 3)$

c $(x - 5)(x - 3)$

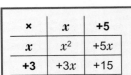

×	x	$+5$
x	x^2	$+5x$
$+3$	$+3x$	$+15$

Answer: $x^2 + 3x + 5x + 15$
Simplify: $\square + \square + \square$

1 **STEM** You can use this formula to calculate the energy, E, of a ball rolling on a flat surface.

$E = \frac{1}{2}mv^2$

where

m = mass of ball (kg) v = speed (metres per second, m/s)

Work out the speed, v, of the ball when

a $E = 9$ and $m = 2$ **b** $E = 8100$ and $m = 200$

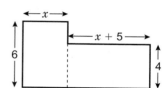
When you know v^2, take the square root to find v. Speed is positive so you can ignore the negative square root.

2 The diagram shows a shape made from two rectangles.
All measurements are in metres.

a Write an expression for the total area of the shape.

b The total area of the shape is $65\,\text{m}^2$.
Write an equation in terms of x, then solve it to find the value of x.

c Work out the perimeter of the shape.

3 You can expand and simplify two sets of double brackets like this.

$$(x + 4)(x + 8) - (x + 2)(x + 5) = [x^2 + 8x + 4x + 32] - [x^2 + 5x + 2x + 10]$$
$$= [x^2 + 12x + 32] - [x^2 + 7x + 10]$$
$$= x^2 + 12x + 32 - x^2 - 7x - 10$$
$$= 5x + 22$$

Expand and simplify $(x + 5)(x + 11) - (x + 3)(x + 7)$.

4 **Problem-solving / Reasoning**

a Show that $(t + 2)(t + 13) - t(t + 17) = (t + 5)(t - 6) - (t - 7)(t + 8)$.

b Explain the method that you used.

5 Make x the subject of each formula.

a $P = x + h$

$P \,\ldots\ldots\ldots = x$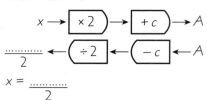

Subtract h from both sides

$x = P \,\ldots\ldots\ldots$

Rewrite with x as the subject on the left-hand side.

b $A = 2x + c$

$x \rightarrow \boxed{\times 2} \rightarrow \boxed{+ c} \rightarrow A$

$\dfrac{\ldots\ldots\ldots}{2} \leftarrow \boxed{\div 2} \leftarrow \boxed{- c} \leftarrow A$

$x = \dfrac{\ldots\ldots\ldots}{2}$

c $T = x - 5y$ **d** $B = 3x - p$ **e** $H = tx - ak$

6 You add numerical fractions by using a common denominator like this:

$\frac{1}{2} + \frac{1}{10} = \frac{5}{10} + \frac{1}{10} = \frac{6}{10} = \frac{3}{5}$

You add algebraic fractions in the same way, so

$\frac{x}{2} + \frac{x}{10} = \frac{5x}{10} + \frac{x}{10} = \frac{6x}{10} = \frac{3x}{5}$

Work out these additions and subtractions. Write each answer in its simplest form.

a i $\frac{1}{2} + \frac{1}{14}$ **ii** $\frac{x}{2} + \frac{x}{14}$

b i $\frac{1}{2} + \frac{5}{6}$ **ii** $\frac{x}{2} + \frac{5x}{6}$

Worked example

7 Complete these.

a $(x^3)^2 = x \,\cdots$

$(x^3)^2 = x^3 \times x^3 = x^{3 \times 2} = x^\square$

b $(x^4)^3 = x \,\cdots$

c $(x^t)^u = x \,\cdots$

8 To expand and simplify an expression with three sets of brackets such as $(x + 3)(x + 1)(x + 2)$, follow these steps.

a First, expand and simplify $(x + 3)(x + 1)$.

It doesn't matter which two brackets you expand first.
Your final expression should have four terms, $x^3 + \square x^2 + \square x + \square$

b Next, multiply your answer to part **a** by $(x + 2)$.

c Finally, simplify your answer to part **b**.

2 Unit test

PROGRESS BAR Colour in the progress bar as you get questions correct. Then fill in the progression chart on pages 104–108.

1 Use the formula $C = kf + t$ to work out the value of C when $k = 3$, $f = 20$ and $t = 32$.

2 Work out the value of these expressions.

    a $3p + q^2$, when $p = 4$ and $q = 5$

    b $(p - q)^3 + 2r$, when $p = 7$, $q = 4$ and $r = 10$

3 A taxi firm charges an amount per person plus an amount per mile travelled.

    a Work out the total charge for 3 people at £5 per person, and a taxi journey of 12 miles at £2 per mile.

    b Write an expression for the total charge for p people at £a per person plus m miles at £b per mile.

    c Write a formula for the total charge, T, in terms of p, a, m and b.

    d Use your formula to work out T when $p = 8$, $a = 2$, $m = 20$ and $b = 3$.

4 Expand and simplify $a(a^2 + 12a) + 5a(3a^2 - 2a)$.

5 Find the value of $p^2(6 - q) - 2r$ when $p = 3$, $q = -4$ and $r = 5$.

6 Factorise each expression completely. Check your answers.

    a $16t + 4$

    b $14t^3 - 4t^5$

    c $t^2 + 8tu + 12st$

    d $6t^2 - 10tw - 2twy$

7 Use the formula $A = pq - X$ to work out the value of

    a A when $p = 4$, $q = 8$ and $X = 12$

    b p when $A = 15$, $q = 2$ and $X = 5$

8 Expand and simplify

    a $(x + 4)(x + 5)$

    b $(x + 2)(x - 6)$

9 Make x the subject of the formula $P = 2x + y$.

10 Complete these.

    a $x^p \times x^q = x^{\cdots\cdots}$

    b $\dfrac{x^p}{x^q} = x^{\cdots\cdots}$

    c $(x^p)^q = x^{\cdots\cdots}$

1 An estate agent wants to find out information about the price of houses in her area in the last year. Which of these ways of collecting information use primary data? ....

> Primary data is data you collect yourself. Secondary data is collected by someone else.

 A She carries out a survey of the customers entering the estate agent's shop.

 B She looks at the office files of houses sold last year.

 C She looks at an internet website showing house prices.

2 For each hypothesis

 i which type of data would you collect to test it?

 ii how would you collect the data?

> A hypothesis is a statement that you can test by collecting data. Different ways of collecting data include questionnaires, surveys, modelling and data logging.

 a 75% of students at my school get a bus to school.

 i primary data

 ii ....

 b Most households have more than one car.

 i ....

 ii look on a website showing average car ownership per household in the UK

3 a A school wants to investigate the length of time students spend doing their maths homework. There are 900 students at the school.

 i Suggest the number of students who should be sampled. ....

 ii What level of accuracy should be used to record their times? ....

> The group of items you test is called the sample.
> The sample must include enough students to give reliable data, but there must be time to ask them. In many cases, 10% of the total population gives a good-sized sample.

 b How will each of these factors affect the data?

 A Asking only students who attend art club. ....

 B Asking only students who attend maths club. ....

 C Asking only students in top set maths. ....

 D Asking only Year 11 students. ....

4 Three people carry out a survey to find out their town's favourite clothes shop.

 Method 1: Tom interviews 50 randomly chosen students at his school.

 Method 2: Alfie stands in the centre of town on a Saturday and asks 250 people that he chooses randomly.

 Method 3: Femka asks her friends, family and neighbours.

> Bias means 'not fair' in some way. In order to reduce bias, your sample must represent the whole population. For example, your sample could be biased if you only ask one age group.

 a Which is the best method and why? ....

 b What bias was there in the other methods?

 Method ____ ....

 Method ____ ....

 c How could you improve the method you chose in part **a**? ....

Guided

CHECK Tick each box as your **confidence** in this topic improves.

Need extra help? Go to page 25 and tick the boxes next to Q1 and 2. Then have a go at them once you've finished 3.1–3.5.

3.2 Collecting data

1 Anti-airplane campaigners want to find out how people feel about using a plane to go on holiday. They ask, 'It is stupid to fly to a holiday when there are lots of great holidays here in the UK, don't you agree?'

a What do you think most people will **answer**? They will agree.

b Why is this a leading question?

The question implies you're stupid if you don't agree.

> A leading question encourages people to give a particular answer.

c Rewrite the question to find out what people really think about using a plane to go on holiday.

> Your question should be precise and should not lead to a particular answer.

2 Here are some records from a dentist's database of patients.

a Design a grouped frequency table to record the patients' ages.

> A grouped frequency table usually has 4 or 5 equal width classes. You can add a tally column for recording the data.

Name	Age	Number of fillings
G. Nasher	23	2
A. Sweet	21	7
C. Risp	59	7
P. Late	39	11
D. Kay	46	11
F. Alsies	56	9
C. Runchie	23	10
B. Race	52	5
D. Rill	56	12
I. N. Jection	60	9
S. Mile	51	3
B. Rush	58	4
C. Rown	63	6
F. Illings	28	6

b i Complete this two-way table to show the number of fillings and the ages of the patients.

		Number of fillings		
		1–5	6–10	11+
Age, a (years)	$20 \leqslant a \leqslant 39$			
	$40 \leqslant a \leqslant 59$			
	60+			

> A two-way table shows data sorted according to two sets of categories.

ii How many patients who are less than 40 years old have 6 or more fillings?

iii What proportion of the patients have between 6 and 10 fillings?

3 Design your own questionnaire to test this hypothesis.

'Most students in Year 8 sleep at least 10 hours on a school night.'

> Think about what data you want to collect, and how you might collect it. Make sure your questions are easily understood and not 'leading'. Check that you can record all possible answers given.

CHECK Tick each box as your **confidence** in this topic improves.

Need extra help? Go to page 25 and tick the box next to Q2. Then have a go at it once you've finished 3.1–3.5.

3.3 Calculating averages

1 a Calculate the mean of 80.2, 89.8, 80.04, 81, 80.5.

b Now calculate the mean using this method.

i Assume the mean is 80.

An assumed mean is an estimated value for the mean, close to all the data values.

Subtract this assumed mean from each of the values. 0.2, 9.8, 0.04, ...

ii Find the mean of your answers to part **b i**.

$$\frac{0.2 + 9.8 + 0.04 + \text{...........................}}{5} = \text{...................}$$

iii Add this value to 80. .... + 80 = ...

Worked example

2 Reasoning / Problem-solving Five even, whole numbers have mode 4, median 8 and mean 8. Work out what they are.

3 a The table shows the heights of a sample of sunflowers. Complete the table.

Height, h (cm)	Frequency	Midpoint of class	Midpoint × Frequency
$0 \leqslant h < 50$	4	$\dfrac{0 + 50}{2} = 25$	25 × 4 = 100
$50 \leqslant h < 100$	13	$\dfrac{50 + 100}{2} = 75$	75 × ....
$100 \leqslant h < 150$	26		
$150 \leqslant h < 200$	7		
Total	50	–	

Use this column to calculate an estimate of the total height for each class.

b What is the modal class? ....

The modal class is the class interval with the highest frequency.

c Work out an estimate for the range.

200 – .... = ...

From the table, what is the smallest possible height of any sunflower?

d Calculate an estimate for the mean height. ....

Divide the sum of the heights by the total number of sunflowers.

4 STEM A botanist is testing the hypothesis that each year a type of mature bamboo is getting taller. She recorded the lengths of 100 of this year's bamboo stems.

a Calculate an estimate for the mean length.

Height, h (cm)	Frequency
$20 < h \leqslant 30$	4
$30 < h \leqslant 40$	17
$40 < h \leqslant 50$	23
$50 < h \leqslant 60$	51
$60 < h \leqslant 70$	5

b Last year the estimate for the mean length was 48.5 cm. Is the botanist's hypothesis correct?

CHECK Tick each box as your confidence in this topic improves.

Need extra help? Go to page 25 and tick the box next to Q3. Then have a go at it once you've finished 3.1–3.5.

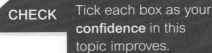

Guided

1 Simon is investigating how much local engineering firms pay their staff.
The grouped frequency table shows the yearly
earnings of staff at one engineering company.

Earnings, e	Number of employees
$0 < e \leq £15\,000$	13
$£15\,000 < e \leq £30\,000$	4
$£30\,000 < e \leq £45\,000$	8
$£45\,000 < e \leq £60\,000$	10

a Draw a frequency polygon for this data.

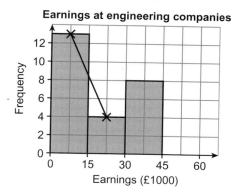

Earnings at engineering companies

First draw a frequency diagram. You can draw
a frequency polygon by joining the midpoints
of the tops of the bars in a frequency diagram.

The second grouped frequency table data
shows yearly earnings at a different engineering
company.

Earnings, e	Number of employees
$0 < e \leq £15\,000$	3
$£15\,000 < e \leq £30\,000$	10
$£30\,000 < e \leq £45\,000$	8
$£45\,000 < e \leq £60\,000$	4

b Construct a frequency polygon for this
data on the axes used in part **a**.

Do you need to draw a frequency
diagram first or can you simply
construct a frequency polygon?

Worked example

c Compare the pay for the two companies.

d How could Simon investigate further?

2 The manager of a shoe shop records
the number of customers and the number
of sales per day for two weeks.
She draws this graph.

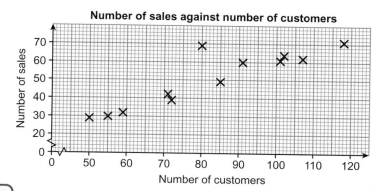

Number of sales against number of customers

a What type of correlation does the graph
show? ....

b Draw a line of best fit.

c Circle an outlier and suggest what
might have caused it.

An outlier is a value that doesn't follow the trend.

d Use the line of best fit to estimate the number
of sales when 65 customers visit. ....

Find 65 on the correct axis. Draw a line up to the
line of best fit and then across to the other axis.

e Use the line of best fit to estimate the number of customers who visited when 50 sales are made.

The manager says, 'About half of all customers buy something.'

f Does the data collected support this statement? ....

g Explain what you would need to do to investigate this statement further.

CHECK Tick each box as your
confidence in this
topic improves.

Need extra help? Go to page 26 and tick
the boxes next to Q4 and 5. Then have a
go at them once you've finished 3.1–3.5.

3.5 Writing a report

1 Real The spreadsheet shows population growth rate from 2012 to 2013 in 10 European countries.

a Use a spreadsheet to draw a bar chart.

b Write two sentences about what the bar chart shows.

	A	B
1	**Country**	**Population growth rate (%)**
2	Ireland	1.50
3	Spain	0.73
4	United Kingdom	0.55
5	France	0.47
6	Italy	0.34
7	Portugal	0.15
8	Belgium	0.05
9	Poland	−0.09
10	Germany	−0.19
11	Bulgaria	−0.81

Source: CIA World Factbook

> How many of these countries have a population that is growing?
> Which population is growing the fastest?
> How many have a decreasing population?
> Which population is decreasing the fastest?

c Explain whether you think your results are a good representation of the population growth rate across the world.

d Describe how you might investigate this further.

> You could investigate how fast the world population is growing.

2 STEM A botanist suggests this hypothesis.

'Tomato plants grow higher when a fertiliser is applied.'

She measures the heights of two groups of tomato plants over a 7-week period.

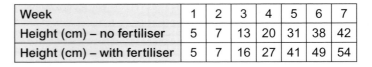

Week	1	2	3	4	5	6	7
Height (cm) – no fertiliser	5	7	13	20	31	38	42
Height (cm) – with fertiliser	5	7	16	27	41	49	54

a Plot two line graphs for this data on the same axes.

b Write a report based on her findings.

Make sure your report answers these questions.
- What do the results show?
- How could she improve her results?
- Do her results give a reliable conclusion?

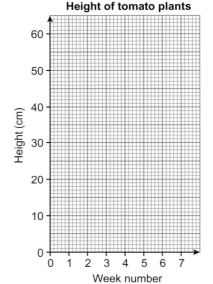

Height of tomato plants

Height (cm) / Week number

c Find the median, range and mean height for both sets of plants.

> A report should include
> - the hypothesis or what you are investigating
> - the data shown in a graph or chart
> - averages and range
> - a conclusion
> - what else you could investigate.

d Write two sentences comparing the two sets of plants.

e Do you think this statement is true? Explain your answer.

'Applying fertiliser increases growth of tomato plants by around 20%.'

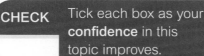

CHECK Tick each box as your **confidence** in this topic improves.

Need extra help? Go to page 26 and tick the box next to Q4. Then have a go at it once you've finished 3.1–3.5.

3 Strengthen

Surveys

1 Gina is doing a social studies investigation on TV viewing.

a She asks 25 people at random in her street.
Is this primary or secondary data?

I collect primary data for my investigation.
Someone else collects secondary data.

b She looks on the internet for UK viewing figures. Is this primary or secondary data?

2 A researcher measures the lengths of a sample of 100 daffodil leaves using a ruler.

a What level of accuracy should the lengths be measured to? ....

A the nearest millimetre   **B** the nearest centimetre   **C** the nearest metre

b The researcher suggests putting the lengths into the following groups.

0–10 cm   10–20 cm   20–30 cm

In which groups could she record a 20 cm long leaf? ....

c What is the problem with her choice of groups? ....

She redesigns her groups.

d Complete the new groups.

0–9 cm   10–.........cm   20–.........cm

Calculating averages

3 John records the length of time he spent in the gym last year.

Guided

Time, t (minutes)	Midpoint	Frequency	Midpoint × Frequency
$0 \leqslant t < 20$	$\dfrac{0 + 20}{2} = 10$	12	$10 \times 12 = 120$
$20 \leqslant t < 40$	$\dfrac{20 + 40}{2} = 30$	15	
$40 \leqslant t < 60$		30	
$60 \leqslant t < 80$		3	
	Total		

The midpoint is an estimate for the average of each class.

a What is the modal class? ....

The modal group contains the most data values.

b Complete the table.

c Which column shows the total number of visits to the gym? ....

d Which column shows the estimated total time? ....

e Work out an estimate for the mean.

It is an estimate because you are using the midpoints to calculate average time.

$$\text{mean} = \frac{\text{total time}}{\text{number of visits to the gym}}$$

Display and analyse

4 George recorded the lengths of some of his runner beans.

Length, l (cm)	Midpoint	Frequency
$10 \leqslant l < 15$	12.5	5
$15 \leqslant l < 20$		25
$20 \leqslant l < 25$		20

a Complete the table.

b Draw a frequency polygon for this data.

Mildred recorded the lengths of some of her runner beans.

Length, l (cm)	Midpoint	Frequency
$10 \leqslant l < 15$		15
$15 \leqslant l < 20$	17.5	20
$20 \leqslant l < 25$		15

c Draw a frequency polygon for this data on the grid used in part **b**.

d Write two sentences comparing the data for each type of runner bean.

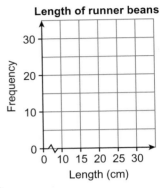

Length of runner beans

5 The scatter graph show the relationship between the maximum daily temperature and the number of visitors to a zoo.

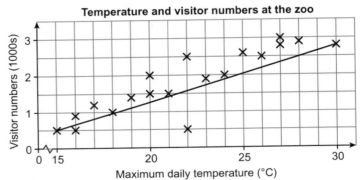

Temperature and visitor numbers at the zoo

a What type of correlation does the graph show? ....

b Put a ring around the data point that is an outlier.

c The line of best fit is not accurate. What has been done incorrectly?

d Draw a line of best fit.

e Predict the number of visitors when the maximum daily temperature is 22°C. ....

f Predict the maximum daily temperature when the number of visitors is 2000. ....

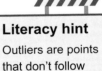

Literacy hint

Outliers are points that don't follow the trend.

Worked example

3 Extend

1 Real An organisation is designing an online survey to find out whether people in a town are happy with the quality of their police force.

Which data should they ask for in the survey? Explain why you did or didn't choose each one.

A name **B** age **C** number of criminal convictions

D years living in the town **E** level of satisfaction with the local police

F ways of improving the quality of their police force

A

B

C

D

E

F

2 Real The owner of a small village shop thinks that the average spend per customer is increasing.

Suggest ways in which she could collect primary data to support her hypothesis.

3 Real Write down the name or URL of a website you might use to investigate the time taken for a satellite to orbit the Earth.

> URL stands for Uniform Resource Locator. It is the web address (e.g. www.pearsonschoolsandfecolleges.co.uk)

4 An athletics club wanted to find out whether athletes who warmed up properly were less likely to injure themselves during training.

90 athletes were surveyed, 12 of whom had injured themselves during training.

Of the 12 who were injured, 9 said they warmed up properly.

Of those who did not injure themselves, 58 said they warmed up properly.

a Construct a two-way table to show this information.

b What do you think the problem might be with a survey like this?

5 Problem-solving Find a possible set of five negative whole numbers that have

mean = −5, median = −5, mode = −5, range = 8

6 STEM A veterinary nurse records the age and mass of kittens.

Age (days)	14	22	21	18	34	25	40	37	41	37	24	20
Mass (g)	170	250	240	220	270	280	390	360	400	380	270	240

a Plot a scatter diagram for this information. Give a title and label the axes.

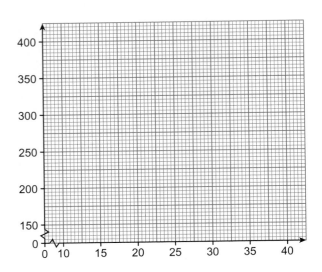

Worked example

b Put a ring around the data point that is an outlier.

   What might be the cause of this outlier?

c Draw a line of best fit on the scatter diagram. Use it to estimate

   i the mass of a kitten which is 30 days old ....

   ii the age of a kitten with a mass of 150 g. ....

d How reliable do you think your answer to part **c ii** is? Explain your answer.

7 Real The tables show the population (in millions) of the UK in 2010 and the projected UK population in 2035.

2010

Age, a (years)	Male	Female
$0 \leqslant a < 20$	7.6	7.2
$20 \leqslant a < 40$	8.4	8.2
$40 \leqslant a < 60$	8.3	8.5
$60 \leqslant a < 80$	5.3	5.9
$80 \leqslant a < 100$	1.1	1.8

2035

Age, a (years)	Male	Female
$0 \leqslant a < 20$	8.4	8.0
$20 \leqslant a < 40$	9.3	8.9
$40 \leqslant a < 60$	9.0	8.7
$60 \leqslant a < 80$	7.2	7.8
$80 \leqslant a < 100$	2.5	3.3

a Write down the modal age group for

   i 2010 ....

   ii 2035. ....

b Calculate an estimate of the mean for

   i 2010 ....

   ii 2035. ....

c Write three sentences comparing the populations of the UK in 2010 and 2035.

3 Unit test

PROGRESS BAR Colour in the progress bar as you get questions correct.
Then fill in the progression chart on pages 104–108.

1 You are going to investigate this hypothesis. 'Drawing pins always land point up.'

How many times should you drop a drawing pin? ☐ 10 times ☐ 100 times ☐ 1000 times

2 A survey asks

How many films have you watched in the last week? ☐ 0–3 ☐ 3–6 ☐ 6–9 ☐ 9+

a Explain what is wrong with the question. ....

b Rewrite the question. ....

3 Selina says, 'At my school, boys can stand on one leg better than girls.'

a What data should Selina collect to test her hypothesis?

b There are 800 students at Selina's school. What sized sample should she use?

c If she timed 20 students standing on one leg, has she found secondary data? Explain.

d Design a frequency table to record her data.

4 The scatter graph shows the height and mass of
some professional footballers.

a What type of correlation does the
graph show? ....

b Ring any outliers.

c Draw a line of best fit.

d Use your line of best fit to estimate the mass of a
1.7 m tall footballer. ....

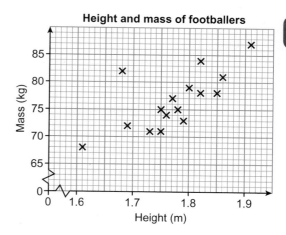

Height and mass of footballers

5 Sam and Mike people record the number of cars
passing their houses every hour for a day.

Sam's data

Number of cars, n	Frequency
$0 \leqslant n < 100$	12
$100 \leqslant n < 200$	10
$200 \leqslant n < 300$	2

Mike's data

Number of cars, n	Frequency
$0 \leqslant n < 100$	4
$100 \leqslant n < 200$	10
$200 \leqslant n < 300$	8

a Which is the modal class for

i Sam's data .... **ii** Mike's data? ....

b Calculate an estimate of the mean for

i Sam's data .... **ii** Mike's data. ....

c Write a sentence comparing the two sets of data.

Guided

1 Enlarge the shape by a scale factor 2 using the centre of enlargement given.

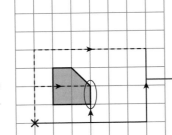

When you enlarge a shape by a scale factor, from a centre of enlargement, the distance from the centre to each point on the shape is also multiplied by the scale factor.

Multiply all the distances from the centre by the scale factor. Count the squares from the centre of enlargement.
• The top of the highlighted line changes from 2 up and 3 right to 4 up and 6 right.
• The bottom of the highlighted line changes from 1 up and 3 right to 2 up and 6 right.

2 **Problem-solving / Reasoning**

   a Draw an enlargement of triangle A with scale factor 2 and centre of enlargement (1, 1).

   b Draw an enlargement of triangle B with scale factor 2 and centre of enlargement (7, 1).

   c What do you notice about your answers to parts **a** and **b**? ....

   d Triangle C has vertices at (3, 6), (5, 6) and (3, 7). Draw triangle C on the grid.

   e Delyth says, 'If I enlarge triangle C by a scale factor of 2 and centre of enlargement (2, 7), it will give exactly the same triangle as my answers to parts **a** and **b**.'
   Is Delyth correct?
   Explain your answer.

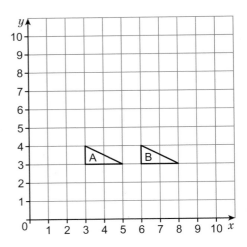

3 Describe the enlargement that takes shape A to shape B in each of these diagrams.

   a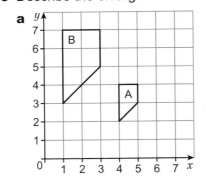

   b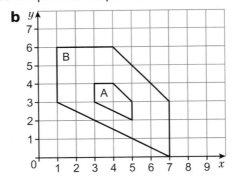

To describe an enlargement, give the scale factor and the coordinates of the centre of enlargement.

CHECK Tick each box as your **confidence** in this topic improves.

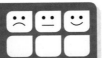

Need extra help? Go to page 35 and tick the box next to Q1. Then have a go at it once you've finished 4.1–4.5.

1 Enlarge the shape using the same marked centre of enlargement and the negative scale factors shown.

> A negative scale factor has the same effect as a positive scale factor except that it takes the image to the opposite side of the centre of enlargement.

a Scale factor −2

b Scale factor −4

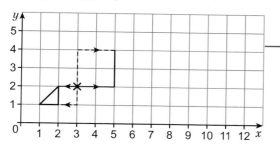

> Count the squares from the centre of enlargement.
> For scale factor of −2
> • the top vertex of the small triangle changes to the bottom vertex of the enlarged triangle, from 1 left to 2 right
> • the bottom right vertex of the triangle changes to the top left vertex of the enlarged triangle, from 1 down and 1 left to 2 up and 2 right.

Guided

2 Enlarge the shapes using the marked centres of enlargement and fractional scale factors.

a scale factor $\frac{1}{2}$

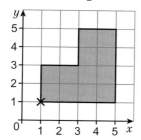

> **Literacy hint**
> We still use 'enlarge' for fractional scale factors, even though they make the shape smaller.

b scale factor $\frac{1}{3}$

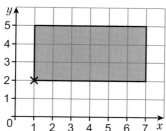

> You can enlarge a shape using a fractional scale factor. Use the same method of multiplying the length of each side by the scale factor.

3 a Enlarge shape A using scale factor $\frac{1}{2}$ and centre of enlargement (7, 0). Label the shape B.

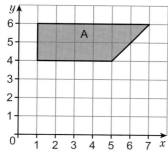

b Write the ratio of the lengths of the sides of shape A to shape B.

c Write the enlargement that will take shape B back to shape A.

> Remember to include the scale factor and the centre of enlargement.

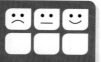

CHECK Tick each box as your **confidence** in this topic improves.

Need extra help? Go to page 35 and tick the box next to Q1. Then have a go at it once you've finished 4.1–4.5.

1 Finance In one year the value of Andy's investments dropped by 5% to £6175. How much were Andy's investments worth at the start of the year?

 Guided

100% − 5% = 95% = 0.95

Original number → $\boxed{\times 0.95}$ → 6175 — $\boxed{\text{Draw a function machine.}}$

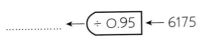

.... ← $\boxed{\div 0.95}$ ← 6175

> You can use inverse operations to find the original amount after a percentage increase or decrease.

Andy's investments were worth .... at the start of the year.

2 Finance / Problem-solving Di bought a pair of trainers for £52. They had been reduced by 20%.

a What was the original price of the trainers before the reduction?

Hammi bought a pair of trainers for £28. They had been reduced by 30%.

b Who saved more money?

> **Worked example**
>
>

3 Finance Wendy invests £2500. A year later the investment is worth £2650. Work out the percentage increase in her investment.

 Guided

Actual change = £2650 − £2500 = £...............

Percentage change = $\dfrac{\text{actual change}}{\text{original amount}} \times 100$

> You can calculate a percentage change using the formula
> percentage change $= \dfrac{\text{actual change}}{\text{original amount}} \times 100$

$= \dfrac{............}{2500} \times 100 = ...\%$

4 Finance Julie invests £7000.
When her investment matures she receives £8540.
Work out the percentage increase in her investment.

> **Literacy hint**
> An investment 'matures' when the investment period (e.g. 5 years) ends.

5 Finance / Real The cost of the London 2012 Olympic and Paralympic Games decreased from an estimated £9.30 billion to a final cost of £8.92 billion. What was the percentage decrease in the estimated cost? Give your answer to the nearest whole number.

> You don't need to write the billions.
> 9.30 − 8.92 = □

CHECK Tick each box as your **confidence** in this topic improves.

Need extra help? Go to page 36 and tick the boxes next to Q8 and 9. Then have a go at them once you've finished 4.1–4.5.

1 Modelling

a A car travels 150 km in 3 hours. Work out the average speed.

$$Speed = \frac{Distance}{Time} = \frac{\text{..........}}{\text{..........}} = \text{..........} \text{ km/h}$$

b A dog runs 100 m in 5 seconds. Work out the average speed.

c Alifa jogs at a speed of 3 m/s. How far does he jog in 30 seconds?

$D = S \times T = \text{..........} \times \text{..........}$

$= \text{..........} \text{ m}$

> Rearrange the formula
> $S = \frac{D}{T}$ to make D the subject.

> Compound measures combine measures of two different quantities. For example, speed is a measure of distance travelled and time taken. It can be measured in metres per second (m/s), kilometres per hour (km/h) or miles per hour (mph). You can calculate average speed if you know the distance and the time.
>
> $Speed = \frac{Distance}{Time}$ or $S = \frac{D}{T}$

d A cyclist travels 90 km at an average speed of 30 km/h. Work out the time taken for the journey.

$T = \frac{\text{..........}}{\text{..........}} = \text{.............................} \text{ hours}$

> How do you need to rearrange the formula?

e Convert 30 km/h to m/s.

f Problem-solving A plane takes off at 0945 and travels 2000 miles at an average speed of 640 km/h. What time does the plane land?

> The distance is in miles, but the speed is in km/h.

2 STEM This table shows the mass, volume and density of three pieces of metal.

a Work out the missing values in the table.

> Density is a compound measure. Density is the mass of substance contained in a certain volume. To calculate it, you need mass in g and volume in cm^3.
>
> $Density = \frac{Mass}{Volume}$ or $D = \frac{M}{V}$
>
> Density is usually measured in grams per cubic centimetre (g/cm^3).

	Mass	Volume (cm³)	Density (g/cm³)
i	312.5 g	25	$\frac{M}{V} = \frac{\text{..........}}{\text{..........}} = \text{..........}$
ii	.... g	40	4.25
iii	15 kg	....	12

b Which is the most dense metal? ....

> Rearrange the formula $D = \frac{M}{V}$ to make M the subject.

3 STEM A force of 48 N is applied to an area of 1.2 m².

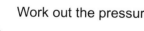

Work out the pressure in N/m². $Pressure = \frac{force (N)}{area (m^2)} = \frac{\text{..........}}{\text{..........}} = \text{..........} \text{ N/m}^2$

4 Real Here are some bottles of fruit juice at different prices from different producers.

a Work out the cost of 10 ml of juice for each bottle.

A
150 ml
90p

B
250 ml
£1.25

C
320 ml
£1.76

b Which bottle is the best value for money? Explain your answer.

Need extra help? Go to pages 35 and 36 and tick the boxes next to Q4, 5, 6 and 7. Then have a go at them once you've finished 4.1–4.5.

1 Finance In 2013 a company's profit fell by 4% to £79.2 million.
What was the company's profit in 2012?

2 Round these numbers to the number of significant figures shown.

> The 4th significant figure is 4, but the 5th digit is 8, so round up.

> You can round numbers to a certain number of significant figures (s.f.). The first significant figure is the one with the highest place value. It is the first non-zero digit in the number, starting on the left.

a 55 348 (4 s.f.) = 55 350

b 0.032 127 (3 s.f.) = 0.0321

> The 3rd significant figure is 1, but the 4th is 2, so leave the 1 as it is.

c 63.349 (4 s.f.) ....

d 39 033 (1 s.f.) ....

e 0.004 33 (2 s.f.) ....

 3 STEM / Modelling The diagram shows the dimensions of a rectangular piece of plastic. A force of 25 N is applied to the piece of plastic.
Work out the pressure in N/cm^2 to 1 significant figure.

15 cm   [rectangle]   40 cm

4 Problem-solving / Reasoning A new hotel is to be built at a scale of 1 : 20 of the height of the Barj Khalifa. The Barj Khalifa is the tallest building in the world and is approximately 800 m high.

a What is the planned height of the new hotel? ....

Each guest is to be given a statue of the new hotel in the scale 1 : 200.

b What is the height of the statue? ....

Adrian says, 'The scale of the statue to the Barj Khalifa is 1 : 220 because 20 + 200 = 220.'

Marshall says, 'The scale of the statue to the Barj Khalifa is 1 : 4000 because 20 × 200 = 4000.'

c Who is correct? Explain your answer. Check your answer by comparing the real height of the Barj Khalifa to your answer in part **b**.

 5 Problem-solving The table shows the numbers of skateboards made in a factory between 2009 and 2013.

Year	2009	2010	2011	2012	2013
Number of skateboards	14 378	16 297	15 205	17 522	17 893

a Work out the percentage increase in skateboard production between 2009 and 2010.
Give your answer to 2 significant figures. ....

b i Between which two years was the smallest percentage increase in skateboard production?

ii What was this percentage increase, to 3 significant figures? ....

c In 2009 each skateboard sold for £19.95. In 2013 each skateboard sold for £24.95.
What was the percentage increase in total takings between 2009 and 2013?
Give your answer to 2 significant figures.

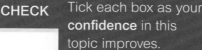 **CHECK** Tick each box as your **confidence** in this topic improves.

Need extra help? Go to page 35 and tick the boxes next to Q2 and 3. Then have a go at them once you've finished 4.1–4.5.

Enlargement

1 Look at the coordinate grid.

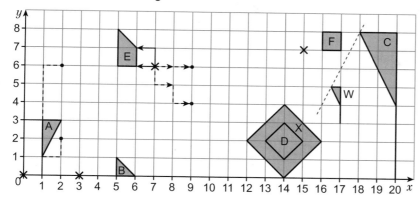

a Enlarge shape A with a scale factor 2 from the centre of enlargement (0, 0). Label your image U.

b Enlarge shape B with a scale factor 3 from the centre of enlargement (3, 0). Label your image V.

> Draw an arrow from the centre to a vertex. Multiply the arrow length by the scale factor. Repeat for other vertices.

c Shape C has been enlarged to shape W. Write down the scale factor and the coordinates of the centre of enlargement. ....

d Shape D has been enlarged to shape X. Write down the scale factor and the coordinates of the centre of enlargement. ....

> Join the corresponding corners of the shapes with straight lines (the first one has been done for you). Make sure the lines are long enough to cross each other.

e Enlarge shape E with a scale factor −2 from the centre of enlargement (7, 6). Label your image Y.

f Enlarge shape F with a scale factor −2 from the centre of enlargement (15, 7). Label your image Z.

> Draw an arrow from the centre to a vertex. Multiply the arrow length by the scale factor. Draw arrows to the new vertex in the opposite direction. Repeat for other vertices.

2 Real A model of the royal yacht Britannia is made using a ratio of 1 : 420. The length of the model is 300 mm.

What is the length of the real ship? Give your answer in

a millimetres ....

b metres. ....

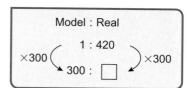

Model : Real

1 : 420

×300 (300 : ☐) ×300

Compound measures

3 Round these numbers to the number of significant figures shown.

a 0.394 (1 s.f.) 0.4

b 0.004 68 (1 s.f.) ....

c 38 499 (2 s.f.) ....

d 6.2781 (3 s.f.) ....

> Circle the first significant figure, 3. It's in the tenths column, so you are rounding to the nearest tenth.
> 0.③94

4 Modelling Complete the table of distance, time and speed.

Distance	Time (hours)	Speed
	2	25 mph
30 miles	3	
250 km	5	
75 km		30 km/h

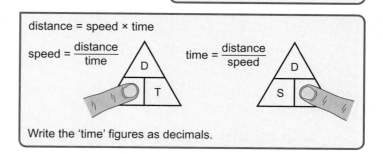

distance = speed × time

$\text{speed} = \dfrac{\text{distance}}{\text{time}}$ $\text{time} = \dfrac{\text{distance}}{\text{speed}}$

Write the 'time' figures as decimals.

35

5 STEM / Modelling Complete the table of mass, volume and density.

Substance	Mass (g)	Volume (cm³)	Density (g/cm³)
Aluminium		25	2.7
Beeswax	62.4		0.96
Carbon	14.04	4	

Cover the quantity you want to find.

6 STEM / Modelling Work out the pressure (N/cm²) when a force of 42 N is applied to an area of 12 cm².

7 Real A pack of 6 bottles costs £1.05. A pack of 9 bottles costs £1.62.

  a Work out the price of 1 bottle in the pack of 6.
    Then work out the price of 9 of these bottles.

÷6 (6 bottles = £1.05) ÷6
    1 bottle = £ ....
×9 (9 bottles = £ ....) ×9

  b Which pack is the better value for money?

Worked example

QR code

Percentage change

8 Work out the original number of members in each of these clubs.

  a Decrease of 20%, down to 28 members

    28 ÷ 80 × 100 = ...

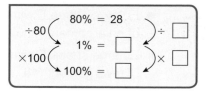

÷80 (80% = 28) ÷ ☐
    1% = ☐
×100 (100% = ☐) × ☐

  b Decrease of 40%, down to 72 members

  c Increase of 10%, up to 55 members

In part **c**, an increase of 10% means you need to start with 110% = 55.

  d Increase of 35%, up to 108 members

9 Zafir invests £5000. When his investment matures he receives £5150.

  a Complete the working to calculate his percentage increase.

    original amount = £5000   actual change = £5150 − £5000 = £150

    percentage change = $\dfrac{\text{actual change}}{\text{original amount}} \times 100 = \dfrac{............}{............} \times 100 = ...$%

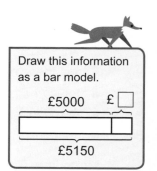

Draw this information as a bar model.

£5000   £ ☐

£5150

  b Check your answer by increasing £5000 by the percentage you calculated. Do you get £5150?

1 Give the scale factor and the centre of enlargement which takes shape A to shape B in these diagrams.

a 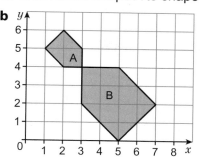 **b**

2 Problem-solving The perimeter of the grey square is 10% greater than the perimeter of the white square.
Work out the side length of the white square.

perimeter = 46.2 m

.........m

3 Problem-solving Between 2011 and 2012 the earnings of a salesman increased by 10%. Between 2012 and 2013 his earnings fell 15%. In 2013 he earned £21 131. How much did he earn in 2011?

Strategy hint

Work out how much he earned in 2012 first.

4 Problem-solving / Modelling A train travels at an average speed of 35 m/s. Work out the time it takes to travel 225 km. Give your answer in hours and minutes, to the nearest minute.

5 Problem-solving / Modelling The block of titanium (A) has a mass of 16.2 kg. The cast iron cube (B) has a density 50% greater than the titanium. Work out the mass of the cast iron cube. Give your answer in grams to 3 significant figures.

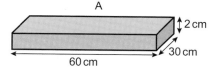

A

2 cm

60 cm   30 cm

B

5 cm

6 Problem-solving Triangles B and C are enlargements of triangle A.

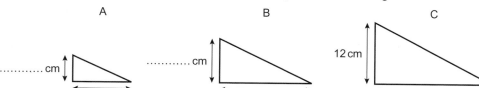

A

.... cm

.... cm

B

.... cm

12 cm

C

12 cm

.... cm

Work out the height of triangle B first, from its area. Then use the ratio of the lengths.

Triangle B has an area of 48 cm². The scale factor of enlargement of the lengths of triangle A to triangle C is 3 : 10. Work out the missing lengths.

7 a Work out the perimeter of the shape.

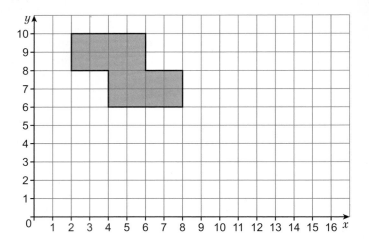

b Transform the shape using an enlargement with scale factor $-\frac{1}{2}$ and centre of enlargement (12, 4). Then reflect the enlargement in the line $x = 9$.

c Use your answer to part **a**, and the scale factor of the enlargement, to work out the perimeter of the final shape. Use the diagram to check that your answer is correct.

8 STEM / Problem-solving The diagram shows a metal square, with a square hole cut out of it.
Work out the force required to create a pressure of 36 N/cm² on the metal.

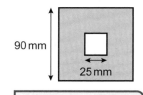

> Work out the area of the metal in cm² first.

9 STEM / Problem-solving The diagram shows a rectangular piece of wood.
When a force of 1830 N is applied to the wood, it creates a pressure of 20 N/cm².
Work out the length, x, of the rectangle.

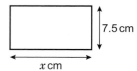

10 STEM / Problem-solving

a Transform the shape using a rotation of 180° about (10, 4), then enlarge by scale factor −2 using centre of enlargement at (13, 5).

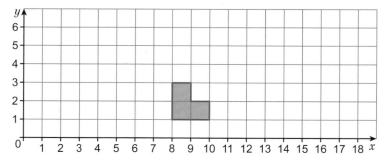

b Describe the single enlargement that will take the finishing shape back to the starting shape.

> Work out the scale factor.
> To find the centre of enlargement use straight lines to join together corresponding corners of the two shapes. Extend these lines across the whole grid. These lines are called rays.

4 Unit test

PROGRESS BAR Colour in the progress bar as you get questions correct.
Then fill in the progression chart on pages 104–108.

1 a Enlarge shape A using the centre of enlargement (2, 3) and a scale factor 2.

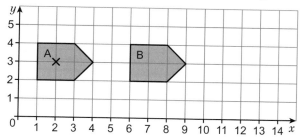

b Describe the enlargement from shape B to your answer to part **a**.

c Enlarge shape B using the centre of enlargement (9, 3) with a scale factor −2.

2 Round these numbers to the number of significant figures shown.

a 44 722 (2 s.f) ....

b 0.0725 (1 s.f.) ....

c 26.772 (3 s.f.) ....

3 In one year the number of members in a table tennis club increases by 20%.
At the end of the year there are 24 members. How many are there at the start of the year?

4 a Neal takes 3 hours to cycle 54 km. Work out his average speed. ....

b Sian walks at an average speed of 4 mph for $2\frac{1}{4}$ hours. How far does she walk? ....

c Rhys drives his speedboat at an average speed of 35 km/h for 28 km. How long does it take him?
Give your answer in minutes.

5 A force of 49 N is applied to an area of 14 cm². Work out the pressure in N/cm².

6 Books of *Scary Stories* are sold in different size multi-packs.

A	B	C
4 Scary Stories £3.28	6 Scary Stories £4.86	10 Scary Stories £8.15

Which pack is the best value for money? Explain your answer.

7 Steve bought a car for £14 000. He sold it for £5600. Work out his percentage loss.

5.1 Using scales

1 Draw a floor plan for the kitchen and utility room of this house.
Use a scale of 1 square to 0.5 m.

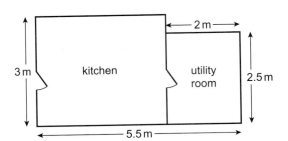

Worked example

2 Real This is a map of the Isle of Wight. Hannah is planning a walking holiday on the island. She thinks the scale of the map is 1 cm for every 2.5 km.

Use Hannah's scale to estimate the distance between

a i Ryde and Sandown

....

ii Totland and Blackgang.

....

Hannah is told that the actual scale of the map is 1 : 300 000.

b What distance in km does 2 cm on the map represent?

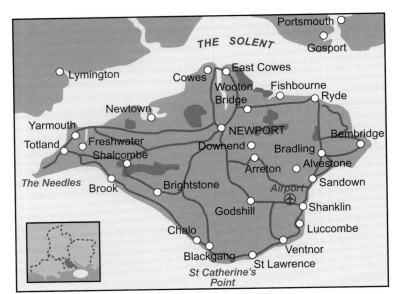

$$600\,000\,\text{cm} \div 100 = 6000\,\text{m} \quad 6000\,\text{m} \div \text{..............} = \text{.......}\,\text{km}$$

c Use the scale 1 : 300 000 to work out the distance between

i Ryde and Sandown

....

....

....

ii Totland and Blackgang.

....

....

....

3 A map has a scale of 1 : 15 000.

What distance on this map represents a real distance of

a 600 m ....

b 3 km ....

c 3.9 km? ....

 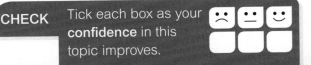

Need extra help? Go to page 44 and tick the boxes next to Q1, 2 and 3. Then have a go at them once you've finished 5.1–5.4.

1 Follow these instructions to construct a perpendicular bisector of the line.

  a Open your compasses greater than half the length of the line. Place the point on one end of the line and draw an arc above and below.

  b Keeping the compasses the same, move them to the other end of the line and draw another arc.

  c Join the points where the arcs intersect. The vertical line divides the horizontal line exactly in half. Do not rub out the arcs.

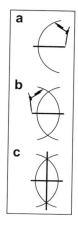

> Construct means draw accurately using ruler and compasses. A perpendicular bisector cuts a line in half at right angles. Bisect means cut in half.

Worked example

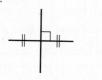

2 Follow these instructions to construct an angle bisector for this 40° angle.

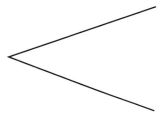

> An angle bisector cuts an angle in half.

  a Open your compasses and place the point at the vertex of the angle. Draw an arc that cuts both arms of the angle.

  b Move the compasses to a point where the arc crosses one of the arms. Make an arc in the middle of the angle.

  c Keep the compasses the same. Do the same from the point where the arc crosses the other arm.

  d Join the point where the arcs cross to the vertex of the angle. The line joins the point where the two small arcs intersect to the point of the angle; it divides the angle exactly in half.

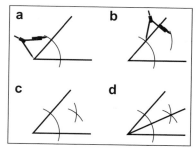

3 Follow these instructions to draw a perpendicular from the point to the line.

  a Put your compasses on the point. Draw an arc that crosses the line segment.

  b Construct the perpendicular bisector of the straight line segment between the arcs.

Worked example

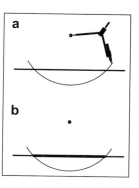

CHECK Tick each box as your **confidence** in this topic improves.

Need extra help? Go to pages 44 and 45 and tick the boxes next to Q4, 5, 6 and 7. Then have a go at them once you've finished 5.1–5.4.

1 Follow these instructions to construct a triangle
with sides of 6 cm, 5 cm and 3 cm.

a Sketch the triangle first.

b Draw a 6 cm line.

c Open your compasses to 5 cm. Place the point
at one end of the 6 cm line. Draw an arc.

d Open the compasses to 2 cm.
Draw an arc from the other end of the 6 cm line.

e Join the intersection of the arcs to each end of the 6 cm line.

3 cm / 5 cm / 6 cm

_____
6 cm

2 A triangle has sides of 3 cm, 7.5 cm and 6 cm.
Construct an accurate drawing of the triangle.

> Always start with a sketch.

Worked example

3 Follow these instructions to construct this right-angled triangle.

a Draw a straight line twice the length of the base (2 × 4 = 8 cm).

b Construct the perpendicular bisector.

c Open your compasses to 5.5 cm (for the sloping side).
Put the point of your compasses at the end of your base line.
Draw an arc to cut the vertical line.

d Join the points.

5.5 cm
4 cm

_____

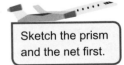

4 The ends of a triangular prism are equilateral triangles of side length 3 cm.
The prism is 2 cm long.

Construct an accurate net for this prism.

> Sketch the prism
> and the net first.

CHECK Tick each box as your
confidence in this
topic improves.

 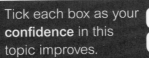

Need extra help? Go to page 46 and tick
the box next to Q8. Then have a go at it
once you've finished 5.1–5.4.

1 Mark two points 6 cm apart. Label them A and B.

a Mark a point that is

   i 3 cm from point A and from point B

   ii 4 cm from point A and from point B

   iii 5 cm from point A and from point B.

b Join the points you have drawn with a line.
What is this line called?

> Use compasses.

A

B

2 Two lines meet at an angle of 80°.
Draw the locus of points equidistant from both lines.

> A locus is a set of all points that obey a rule. Often this gives a path. The plural of locus is loci.

> **Literacy hint**
> Equidistant means 'the same distance from a point'.

> First draw the 80° angle and then construct the angle bisector.

3 **Problem-solving** Two mobile phone masts are 10 km apart.

Each mast transmits 6 km in any direction.

a Draw a scale diagram to show clearly the range of each mast. Use a scale of 1 cm : 1 km.

b Shade the locus of the area that has a phone signal from both masts.

The mobile phone company wants to decrease the range of its transmitters.

c What would each transmitter's new range need to be to make sure that everybody living on a straight line between them will get a phone signal?

> What shape do the points that are 6 km away in any direction make?

> **Worked example**
>

CHECK Tick each box as your **confidence** in this topic improves.

Need extra help? Go to page 46 and tick the boxes next to Q9 and 10. Then have a go at them once you've finished 5.1–5.4.

Using scales

1 Daniel has designed a piece of modern art for the school magazine. Make an accurate drawing of the art.
Use a scale of 1 cm to 2 cm.

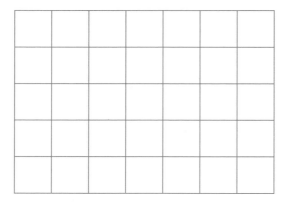

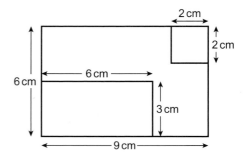

Use a double number line.

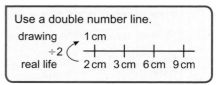

2 Gina's garden is shown in this plan.

The scale is 1 cm to 4 m.

Write down the lengths of the sides of her garden.

short side = 4 cm, 4 × 4 m = 16 m

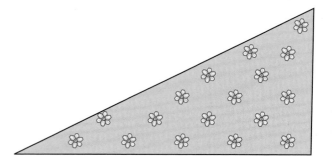

3 A map has a scale of 1 : 200 000.

a A distance is 7 cm on the map. How far is it in real life?

b A distance is 3.2 cm on the map. How far is it in real life?

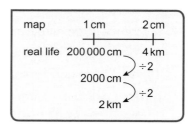

Basic constructions

4 Follow these instructions to construct the perpendicular bisector of this line.

a Draw the first arc.

b Draw the second arc.

c Draw the perpendicular bisector.

Remember this diagram.

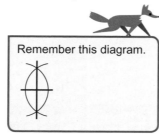

5 a Draw a line at an angle of 50° to the line.

Sketch what you think it will look like first.

_____

b Follow the instructions to construct the bisector of this angle.

i Draw an arc. **ii** Draw the first arc between the two sides of the angle. **iii** Draw the second arc. **iv** Draw the angle bisector.

6 Construct the bisector of this angle.

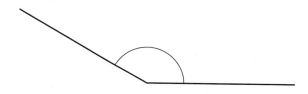

Worked example

7 Follow the instructions below to construct a perpendicular line from the point A to the line.

A

_____

a Draw an arc from point A.

b Keep your compasses the same distance apart. Draw an arc from each of the two points where the arc crosses the line.

c Join the points where the arcs intersect.

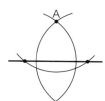 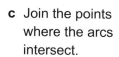 

Constructing triangles

8 Follow these instructions to construct accurately a triangle with sides 3 cm, 4 cm and 6 cm.

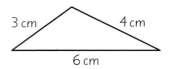

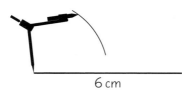

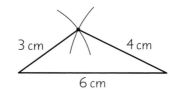

a Open your compasses to exactly 3 cm and draw an arc from the left-hand end of the line.

b Open your compasses to exactly 4 cm and draw an arc from the other end of the line.

c Use the point where the arcs cross to create the finished triangle.

Loci

9 Draw an accurate diagram to show all the points 3 cm away from the point X.

Use compasses

X •

Worked example

10 Two ants are standing 4 cm apart.

A third ant walks between them, the same distance away from each of them.

Construct a diagram to show the route of the third ant.

Worked example

46

1 The sketched diagram shows a radio mast and two of its wires.

   a Construct an accurate diagram. Use a scale of 1 cm to 10 m.

   b How tall is the mast?

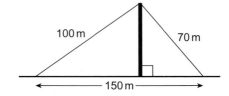

2 A map has a scale of 1 : 125 000. Fatima says that 4 km is represented by 5 cm. Is she right? Show your working.

3 A ship leaves a port and sails west for 10 km before turning and sailing north for 4 km. Use construction to work out how far away is the ship from the port.

4 Construct an angle of precisely 22.5°.

Construct a right angle, bisect it, then bisect again.

5 Construct an equilateral triangle of side length 4 cm.

6 The sketch shows the loci of two water sprinklers on a lawn. The sprinklers are 6 m apart. Sprinkler A has a range of 4 m, and sprinkler B has a range of 3 m. Construct an accurate scale drawing and shade in the region that gets the most water.

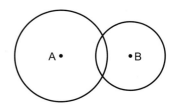

7 A scale drawing of a cinema screen has scale 1:24. The length of the drawing is 63 cm. What is the length of the real cinema screen? Give your answer in metres, correct to 1 decimal place.

Worked example

8 A model of a ship is to be made using a scale of 1:80. The ship is 200 m long. How long is the model? Give your answer in centimetres.

5 Unit test

PROGRESS BAR Colour in the progress bar as you get questions correct.
Then fill in the progression chart on pages 104–108.

1 Draw a line segment of 7 cm.

Use a ruler and compasses to construct the
perpendicular bisector of the line segment.

2 Construct the angle bisector of this angle.

3 The point A lies 4 cm away from a straight line.

Construct a perpendicular line from this point to the line.

A •

4 A map has a scale of 1 : 40 000.

a What distance in real life is represented by a distance of 3.5 cm on the map?

b The distance between two towns is 16 km. How far will this distance be on the map?

5 The diagram shows a plank of wood leaning on a wall.

a Construct an accurate scale drawing of the diagram.

b How far up the wall does the ladder reach?

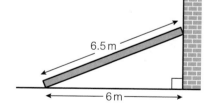

6.5 m

6 m

6 Two water sprinklers are 9 m apart.

One sprinkler has a range of 5 m. The other sprinkler has a range of 3 m.

Show that there is an area not watered by both sprinklers.

5.5 cm

4 cm

1 Solve these equations.

Guided

a $\dfrac{2x + 1}{3} = 5$

$\dfrac{3(2x + 1)}{3} = 3 \times 5$

> This equation has a fraction on one side. Multiply both sides by the denominator.

$\dfrac{\cancel{3}(2x + 1)}{\cancel{3}} = 3 \times 5$

> Cancel the 3 ÷ 3

$2x + 1 = 15$

$2x = \ldots\ldots\ldots$

$x = \ldots\ldots\ldots$

LHS: If $x = \ldots\ldots$

$\dfrac{2 \times \ldots\ldots + 1}{3} = \dfrac{\ldots\ldots + 1}{3} = \dfrac{\ldots\ldots}{3} = 5$

$= $ RHS ✓

> Substitute your solution back into the original equation. If it is correct, both sides of the equation will have the same value.

b $\dfrac{2x + 1}{5} = x - 7$

> Multiply both sides by the denominator. Then cancel, expand the bracket, and solve.

2 Ed and Marie start with the same number. Ed doubles this number, adds 2 and then divides the result by 2. Marie multiplies the number by 3 and then subtracts 9. They both get the same answer.
What number did they start with?

> **Strategy hint**
> Use a letter for the number. Write expressions for Ed and Marie's calculations.

3 Solve the equation $x^2 + 8 = 72$.

Guided

$x^2 = 72 - \ldots\ldots\ldots$

$x^2 = \ldots\ldots\ldots$

$x = \ldots\ldots\ldots$

4 Find the value of x.

> **Strategy hint**
> Write an equation using the area.

a

x | area = 144

x

b

2

5

x | area = 71

x

5 Solve these equations.

a $-2(x - 5) = 19 + x$

b $3(2t - 3) = 31 - 2(2t - 5)$

> Collect like terms wherever you can.

CHECK Tick each box as your **confidence** in this topic improves.

Need extra help? Go to page 56 and tick the boxes next to Q1 and 2. Then have a go at them once you've finished 6.1–6.6.

1 State whether each of these is an expression (Ex), equation (Eq), function (Fu) or formula (Fo).

a $E = mc^2$ ....

b $3a + b$ ....

c $x \rightarrow \frac{1}{2}x + 2$ ....

d $2t - 6 = 14$ ....

> An expression has numbers and letters but no equals sign.
> An equation has two expressions, or an expression and a number, on either side of an equals sign. When there is only one letter, you can solve it to find the unknown value.
> A formula is a rule that shows a relationship between two or more variables (letters). You can use substitution to find each unknown value.
> A function is a rule that changes one number into another. $x \rightarrow 3x + 4$ is a function.

2 a Which of these are true for all values of x and which are true for only some values of x or for just one value?

i $x - 3 = 7$ ....

ii $2x + 5 = 5 + 2x$ ....

iii $4 + 4x = 8x$ ....

iv $4x + 12 = 4(x + 3)$ ....

v $16x^2 = (4x)^2$ ....

vi $x^2 = 9x$ ....

b Rewrite any one of the identities using $\equiv$. ....

> An identity is an equation that is true for all values of the variables. The $\equiv$ sign shows an identity.
> For example, $0.5x \equiv \frac{x}{2}$ and $2x \equiv x + x$ are identities.

3 Use the correct sign, $=$ or $\equiv$.

a $x + x + x$ ..... $3x$

b $6x + 3$ ..... 9^2

c $5t + 6$ ..... $2 + 7t + 4 - 2t$

4 Change these recurring decimals into fractions.

a $0.\dot{4} = 0.444\,44... = n$ — Call the recurring decimal n.

$n = 0.444\,44...$, so $10n = 4.444\,44...$ — Multiply the recurring decimal by 10.

$10n - n = 4.444\,44... - 0.444\,44...$ — Subtract the value of n from the value of $10n$ so you get all decimal places zero.

$9n = 4$ — Solve the equation.

$n =$ ....

b $0.\dot{5}$

> All recurring decimals can be written as fractions.

5 Change these recurring decimals into fractions.

a $0.\dot{7}\dot{9}$

b $0.2\dot{4}$

c $0.7\dot{5}$

d $0.34\dot{5}$

> In part **b**, there is one recurring digit, so multiply by 10. Be careful when solving the equation.

Strategy hint

Multiply by a multiple of 10. Try $10n$ or $100n$ or $1000n$.

Worked example

CHECK Tick each box as your **confidence** in this topic improves.

Need extra help? Go to page 56 and tick the box next to Q4. Then have a go at it once you've finished 6.1–6.6.

51

1 Substitute $x = 4$ and $x = 5$ into the expression $\frac{5x}{3}$. Which value gives an answer closer to 7?

2 Use trial and improvement to find a solution to these equations.
Give your answer to 1 decimal place.

> **Strategy hint**
> Draw your own table.

a $x^3 = 50$ — Draw a table. Use a calculator to try values of x.

b $x^3 + 4 = 15$

$x^3 = 15 - 4$ — Simplify the equation if possible.

$x^3 = 11$

Guided

x	x^3	Comment
3	27	too small
4	64	too big
3.5	42.875	too small
3.6	46.656	too small
3.7	50.653	too big

x is between 3.6 and ....

3.7^3 (50.653) is closer to 50 than 3.6^3 (46.656)

so $x =$ .... (1 d.p.).

> Find the two values to 1 d.p. that x is between. Decide which is closer to x.
>
> 46.656   50.653
>
> 46   47   48   49   (50)   51

3 Use trial and improvement to find the value of x (to 1 decimal place) in these equations.

a $x^2 + x = 47$

x	$x^2 + x$	Comment
6	42	

b $x^3 - x = 66$

c $x^3 + 5x = 160$

> **Worked example**
>
>

CHECK Tick each box as your **confidence** in this topic improves.

Need extra help? Go to page 57 and tick the box next to Q5. Then have a go at it once you've finished 6.1–6.6.

Guided

1 Show these inequalities on a number line.
Find the integer values that satisfy each one.

Literacy hint

'Satisfy' means make the statement true.

You can also show solutions on a number line.
An empty circle shows that the value is not included.

○

A filled circle shows that the value is included.

●

An arrow shows that the solution continues towards infinity.

○———→

a $x > 3$

integers: 4, 5, 6, …

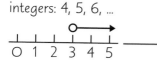

This includes all the numbers greater than 3 (*excluding* 3).

b $x \leqslant 7$

integers: 7, 6, 5, 4, …

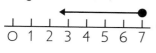

This includes all the numbers less than or equal to 7 (*including* 7).

c $x > 5$

d $x \geqslant -2$

e $3 < x \leqslant 6$

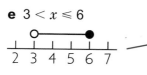

This includes all the numbers greater than 3 and less than or equal to 6.

f $4 \leqslant x < 7$

2 Solve these inequalities.
Show each solution on a number line.

You can solve inequalities in a similar way to solving equations. Use the balancing method of doing the same to both sides of the inequality to solve it. When you multiply or divide by a negative number, change the direction of the inequality sign.

a $x + 6 > 10$

$x >$ ....   Subtract 6 from both sides.

b $x - 4 < 8$

c $5x \geqslant 20$ Divide by 5, just as you would do if you were solving an equation.

d $2x + 4 > 20$

e $\dfrac{x}{5} < 10$

Worked example

3 Solve these inequalities.

a $10 - x < 14$

$-x < 4$ Subtract 10 from both sides.

$0 < 4 + x$ Add x to both sides.

$-4 < x$ Subtract 4 from both sides.

or $x > -4$

b $-3x < 15$

c $-\dfrac{x}{5} > 2$

4 Solve these inequalities. Show each solution on a number line.

a $2(x + 5) > 16$

b $3(x - 4) < -6$

c $10 > 5(x - 3)$

CHECK Tick each box as your **confidence** in this topic improves.

Need extra help? Go to page 56 and tick the box next to Q3. Then have a go at it once you've finished 6.1–6.6.

1 STEM In a science experiment Dermot measures how far a spring extends when he adds different masses to it.
The table shows his results.

Mass, m	100 g	200 g	300 g	400 g	500 g
Extension, e	20 cm	40 cm	60 cm	80 cm	100 cm

a Do Dermot's results show a proportional relationship between m and e?

b Write a formula that shows this relationship between mass (m) and extension (e).

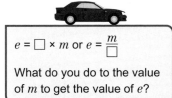

$e = \square \times m$ or $e = \dfrac{m}{\square}$

What do you do to the value of m to get the value of e?

c Use your formula to predict how far the wire will stretch with a mass of 150 g.

2 Check whether each of these quantities are varying in direct proportion.

a 8 brushes cost 48p, 22 cost £1.32

b 10 pens cost £4, 25 cost £10

c 6 planks weigh 12 kg, 14 weigh 40 kg

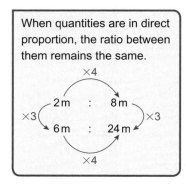

When quantities are in direct proportion, the ratio between them remains the same.

$\times 4$

$\times 3 \bigg($ 2 m : 8 m $\bigg) \times 3$

6 m : 24 m

$\times 4$

3 The values of P and Q are in direct proportion. Work out the missing numbers A, B, C and D.

Value of P	12	18	16	C	D ....
Value of Q	27	A	B	18	22.5

4 Real On a particular day, £30 will buy 1500 Russian roubles.
The number of roubles (R) varies in proportion to the number of pounds (P).
How many Russian roubles can I buy with £1000?

$y \propto x$ means 'y is proportional to x'.

Guided

This means that $R \propto P$, or $R = kP$ ──── Write the proportional relationship as an equation with a constant of proportionality, k.

$R = 1500$ and $P = 30$, so $1500 = k \times 30$

So $k = 50$ and $R = 50P$ ──── Substitute the values into the equation. Solve the equation to find k, and rewrite it using the value of k.

Substitute $P = 1000$

$R = 50 \times 1000 = $ ....

So £1000 can buy .... Russian roubles. ──── Use your equation to answer the question.

5 Real On a particular day, £40 will buy 6800 Japanese yen.
The number of yen (Y) varies in proportion to the number of pounds (P).
How many Japanese yen can I buy with £500?

CHECK Tick each box as your **confidence** in this topic improves.

Need extra help? Go to page 57 and tick the box next to Q6. Then have a go at it once you've finished 6.1–6.6.

6.6 Simultaneous equations

1 Solve these pairs of simultaneous equations.

a $3x + y = 21$ ①

$y = 4x$ ②

> Write one equation above the other with the equals signs lined up. Number them ① and ②.

$3x + 4x = 21$

$7x = 21$

$x = 3$

> Substitute the value of y from equation ② into equation ①. Then simplify and solve.

b $2x + y = 25$ ①

$y = 3x$ ②

Substitute into equation ②

$y = 4 \times 3$

$y = \ldots\ldots$

> Substitute the value of x into one equation. Choose the simpler one to solve.

Check: $3x + y = 21$ ①

$3 \times 3 + \ldots\ldots = 21$ ✓

> Check the values in the other equation.

2 Solve these pairs of simultaneous equations.

a $2x + y = 7$ ①

$+ \quad 5x - y = 14$ ②

$\overline{7x + O = 21}$

$x = 3$

> Add equations ① and ② together, then solve.

b $4x - 3y = 7$

$x + 3y = 13$

> You can add whole equations together to help solve simultaneous equation problems.

Substitute $x = 3$ into equation ①

$2 \times 3 + y = 7$

$y = \ldots\ldots$

> Substitute $x = 3$ into one equation.

Check: $5x - y = 14$ ②

$5 \times 3 - \ldots\ldots = 14$ ✓

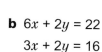

3 Solve these pairs of simultaneous equations.

a $4x + y = 12$ ①

$6x + y = 18$ ②

$2x = 6$

> Subtract ① from ②.

$x = \ldots\ldots$

> Substitute the value for x into one of the equations.

b $6x + 2y = 22$

$3x + 2y = 16$

Worked example

4 Problem-solving John buys 2 T-shirts and 6 jumpers for £85.
Terry buys 2 T-shirts and 3 jumpers for £47.50.
How much are T-shirts and jumpers?

> Subtract one equation from the other.

CHECK Tick each box as your **confidence** in this topic improves.

Need extra help? Go to page 57 and tick the box next to Q7. Then have a go at it once you've finished 6.1–6.6.

55

6 Strengthen

Solving equations and inequalities

1 a Work out

    i $(-3)^2$ ....   **ii** 3^2 ....

    iii $(-4)^2$ ....   **iv** 4^2 ....

> $(-3)^2 = -3 \times -3$

> Notice that $(-3)^2$ and 3^2 give the same answers and $(-4)^2$ and 4^2 give the same answers.

b Solve these equations. Give both possible values of x.

    i $x^2 = 64$

        $x =$ ....

> What numbers square to give 64?

    ii $x^2 + 3 = 28$

> Rearrange to get x^2 on its own.

2 Solve these equations.

Guided

a $\dfrac{3x + 4}{2} = x + 5$

$\dfrac{2(3x + 4)}{2} = 2(x + 5)$

$3x + 4 = 2x + 10$

> Use brackets to multiply all the terms on the right-hand side.

b $\dfrac{5x + 4}{2} = 4x + 5$

3 Solve these inequalities and show each one on a number line.

a $x + 8 > 12$

> Subtract 8 from both sides.

b $x - 5 \leqslant 1$

c $2x + 4 < 10$

d $2(x + 3) \geqslant 26$

> Expand the brackets first.

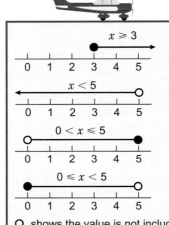

$x \geqslant 3$

0 1 2 3 4 5

$x < 5$

0 1 2 3 4 5

$0 < x \leqslant 5$

0 1 2 3 4 5

$0 \leqslant x < 5$

0 1 2 3 4 5

○ shows the value is not included.
● shows the value is included.

4 Change these recurring decimals into fractions.

Guided

a $0.\dot{2}$

$n = 0.222...$

$10n = 2.222...$

> Work out $10n - n$, so you have an equation for $9n = \square$. Then rearrange to have $n = \square$.

b $0.\dot{3}\dot{1}$

$n = 0.3131...$

$100n =$ ....

> Two digits are repeated, so multiply by 100 and then use the same process as in part **a**.

Trial and improvement

Guided

5 a Use trial and improvement to solve these to 1 decimal place.

i $x^2 = 70$

x	x^2	Comment
9	81	too big
8	64	too small
8.5	72.25	too big
8.4	70.56	too big
8.3	....	too ....
8.35	....	too ....

Halfway between 8.3 and 8.4 is 8.35.

ii $x^3 + 10 = 83$

Work out which two consecutive whole numbers the answer lies between. One must be 'too small', the other 'too big'. Then work out which two consecutive 1 d.p. numbers the answer lies between.

b Complete the number line using your trial and improvement table.

i
```
  68.89   .........   .........
  ---+-------+-------+---
    8.3    8.35    8.4
```

ii
```
    .........   .........   .........
  ----+---------+---------+----
    .........   .........   .........
```

c Shade the part of the line where x must be. What do all the values in this part round to, to 1 d.p?

i ....

ii ....

Proportion

Guided

6 X and Y are in direct proportion. Work out the missing numbers P and Q.

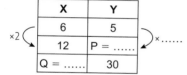

X	Y
6	5
12	P = ...
Q = ...	30

×2   × ......

Simultaneous equations

Guided

7 Find the values of x and y that satisfy these pairs of equations.

a $4x + y = 14$

$y = 3x$

$4x + 3x = 14$ ——— Replace the y in the first equation with $3x$ from the other equation.

$....... x = 14$ ——— Simplify and solve.

$x = ...$

$y = 3 × ....$ ——— Use $x = \square$ to substitute into the second equation to work out the value of y.

$y = ...$

b $5x + y = 20$

$3x - y = 4$

c $4x + 2y = 32$

$4x - 2y = 8$

Strategy hint

In parts **b** and **c**, adding both equations together will cancel out y. Remember to add all like terms together.

1 Solve these equations.

a $\dfrac{4x + 2}{5} = -2x + 6$

b $\dfrac{-4x + 6}{9} = -4 - 2x$

2 Solve these equations.

a $\dfrac{5x}{2} = \dfrac{2}{3}$

b $\dfrac{6x + 1}{5} = \dfrac{3x - 2}{2}$

3 This table shows distances between friends' houses, in miles and km.

a Calculate the missing distances A and B.

b It takes Hassan 1 hour 15 minutes to drive from Bolton to Bradford.
Work out his average speed in

i miles per hour

ii metres per second.

From	To	Miles	Kilometres
Bolton	Bradford	45	72
Swansea	Truro	235	A ....
Penrith	Hartlepool	B	120

4 The formula $s = \dfrac{u + v}{2}$ is used to calculate the average velocity of an object where s is the average velocity, u is the initial velocity and v is the final velocity.

The average velocity of an object was 6 m/s and the initial velocity was 2 m/s. What was the final velocity of the object?

Literacy hint

Velocity is the speed of an object in a certain direction. The initial velocity is the starting velocity.

5 For each equation, use trial and improvement to find the value of x to 2 decimal places.

a $x^3 + 5x = 76$

x	$x^3 + 5x$	Comment
3.8	73.872	too small
3.9	78.819	too ....
3.85	76.316...	too ....
3.84	75.823...	too ....
3.845	....	too ....

The solution is between 3.84 and 3.85. You need to know which is closer, so try the number halfway between them, 3.845.

3.845 is too big. This means that the solution must be closer to the smaller of the two numbers, 3.84.

The solution is .... to 2 decimal places.

b $x^3 + 2x = 84$

6 In each of these questions, $y = kx^2$. Give each value of y to 2 decimal places.

   a When $y = 3$, $x = 5$.

     What will be the value of y when $x = 10$?

     $3 = k \times 5^2$, so $k = \dfrac{3}{25}$, so $y = \dfrac{3}{25}x^2$ —— | Substitute 10 for x to work out the value of y. |

   b When $y = 4$, $x = 14$. What will be the value of y when $x = 22$?

7 $x + 3y = 7$ and $6x - 3y = 21$ are a pair of simultaneous equations.

   a Add the equations together.

   b What happens to the y terms? ....

   c Solve your equation for x.

   d Using the value of x, find the value of y.

8 Problem-solving Gina's parent's ages sum to 65 years and have a difference of 9 years.
How old are Gina's parents?

| Create a pair of simultaneous equations that represent this situation. |

6 Unit test

PROGRESS BAR Colour in the progress bar as you get questions correct. Then fill in the progression chart on pages 104–108.

1 Write whether each of these is an expression (Ex), equation (Eq), function (Fu) or formula (Fo).

a $F = ma$ .... **b** $x \rightarrow 5x$ .... **c** $2x - 3 = 7$ .... **d** $2a + 9$ ....

2 Write the sign, = or ≡, to make each statement correct.

a $4x + 3$ .... 9 **b** $6x + 2x$ .... $8x$ **c** $5(x - 2)$ .... $5x - 10$

3 Solve these equations.

a $\dfrac{5x - 2}{4} = 2x - 8$ **b** $x^2 + 7 = 88$

4 The values of x and y are in direct proportion.
Use the equality of ratios to find the missing values, A and B.

x	8	A	30
y	32	20	B ....

5 Solve the inequality. Show the solution on a number line.

$2x + 3 > 11$

6 Solve this pair of simultaneous equations.

$2x + 3y = 16$
$3x - 3y = 9$

7 Convert the recurring decimal $0.\dot{2}\dot{9}$ to a fraction.

8 $x = ky^2$

a Use the first pair of values in the table to find k.

x	300	A	1200
y	5	6	B ....

b Work out the missing values, A and B, in the table.

1 a The radius of a circular mirror is 12 cm.
Work out its diameter.

$d = 2 \times r = 2 \times$ .... = ... cm

b The diameter of a bicycle tyre is 52 cm.
Work out its radius.

$r = d \div 2 =$ .... $\div 2 =$ .... cm

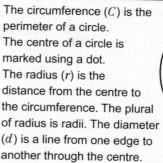

The circumference (C) is the perimeter of a circle.
The centre of a circle is marked using a dot.
The radius (r) is the distance from the centre to the circumference. The plural of radius is radii. The diameter (d) is a line from one edge to another through the centre.

diameter, d centre   radius, r

circumference, C

2 Real / Reasoning The table shows the diameters and approximate circumferences of some jar lids.

The Greek letter π (pronounced pi) is a special number 3.141 592 653 5…
To find the circumference C of a circle with diameter d, use the formula $C = \pi d$.
If you know the radius r you can use the equivalent formula $C = 2\pi r$.
Use the π key on your calculator.

Diameter, d (mm)	Circumference, C (mm)	$\dfrac{C}{d}$
35	110	
56	176	
86	270	

a Complete the table. Round the values of $\dfrac{C}{d}$ to 2 decimal places.

b What do you notice about the value of $\dfrac{C}{d}$? What does this mean?

c Complete the formula $C =$ .... $\times d$.

d Use your formula to estimate the circumference of a jar lid with diameter 40 mm.

3 Work out the circumference of this circle.
Round your answer to an appropriate degree of accuracy.

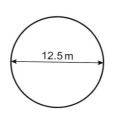

12.5 m

12.5 m is measured to 1 decimal place so your answer should have the same degree of accuracy.

4 a Work out, to 2 significant figures, the diameter of a circle with a circumference of 30 cm.

Start by writing the value you know in the formula $C = \pi d$.

Worked example

b Work out, to 2 significant figures, the radius of a circle with a circumference of 200 m.

5 Problem-solving The diagram shows a semicircular pattern.
Work out the total length of the black lines, including all of the radii.

Literacy hint

Half a circle is called a semicircle.

Find the circumference of half a circle. Add the diameter and the other two radii.

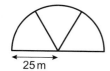

25 m

CHECK   Tick each box as your **confidence** in this topic improves.

Need extra help? Go to page 66 and tick the boxes next to Q1 and 2. Then have a go at them once you've finished 7.1–7.5.

61

1 Work out the area of each circle.
Round your answers to an appropriate degree of accuracy.

a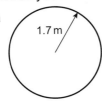
1.7 m

b
320 mm

The formula for the area A of a circle with radius r is $A = \pi r^2$. Use the π key on your calculator.

Guided

Area $= \pi r^2 = \pi \times 1.7^2$
$= 9.079...$
$= 9.1 \, m^2$

2 **Problem-solving / Modelling** The diagram shows a metal sheet with four circles cut from it.
Work out the area of the remaining metal.

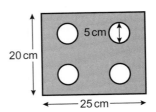
20 cm
5 cm
25 cm

Worked example

Strategy hint
First calculate the area of one hole.

3 Work out the area of each shape. Give your answers in terms of π.

a
8 cm

b
12 m

Area of a circle of radius 5 m is $A = \pi r^2 = \pi \times 5^2 = 25\pi \, m^2$ in terms of π.

4 Work out the perimeter of the quarter circle in Question 3.

5 Work out the radii of circles with these areas. Write your answers using appropriate units and to a sensible degree of accuracy.

a $4 \, m^2$ **b** $4500 \, km^2$

Strategy hint
Start by writing the values you know in the formula for area.

Guided

Area $= \pi r^2$
$4 = \pi \times r^2$ so $r^2 = 4 \div \pi$
$r = \sqrt{\rule{3cm}{0pt}} = \rule{3cm}{0pt}$

6 **STEM / Modelling** A radio station mast emits a signal in all directions that covers an area of up to $17\,000 \, km^2$.

a How far from the mast does the signal reach?
Write your answer to an appropriate degree of accuracy.

Strategy hint
Draw a diagram.

b How reliable is the model you used?

CHECK Tick each box as your **confidence** in this topic improves.

Need extra help? Go to page 66 and tick the boxes next to Q3, 4 and 5. Then have a go at them once you've finished 7.1–7.5.

1 Write the length of the hypotenuse for this triangle.

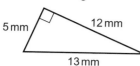

5 mm   12 mm
13 mm

> The longest side of a right-angled triangle is called the hypotenuse.

hypotenuse = ...

2 Work out the length of the hypotenuse in each of these right-angled triangles, correct to the nearest mm.

Guided

a
a
4 mm c
6 mm
b

> Label the hypotenuse c and the other sides a and b.

b
12 mm
8 mm

$c^2 = a^2 + b^2$

$= 4^2 + 6^2$

> Substitute $a = 4$ and $b = 6$ into the formula for Pythagoras' theorem, $c^2 = a^2 + b^2$. Then solve the equation.

$= 16 + \text{......} = \text{......}$

$c = \sqrt{\text{......}} = \text{...........}$ mm

$= \text{......}$ mm to the nearest mm

> Pythagoras' theorem shows the relationship between the lengths of the three sides of a right-angled triangle.
>
>
> $c^2 = a^2 + b^2$

Worked example

3 Work out the length of the unknown side of each right-angled triangle. Give your answers to an appropriate degree of accuracy.

Guided

a
a
6 cm c
9 cm
b

b
3.5 cm   4.2 cm

> **Strategy hint**
>
> Label the hypotenuse c and the other sides a and b. Substitute into Pythagoras' theorem, $c^2 = a^2 + b^2$. Then solve the equation.

$c^2 = a^2 + b^2$

$9^2 = 6^2 + b^2$

$9^2 - \text{......}^2 = b^2$

$b = \sqrt{\text{......}} = \text{...................}$

4 Problem-solving The diagram shows a field in the shape of an isosceles trapezium.
The measurements are correct to the nearest metre.
Work out the area of the field in km².

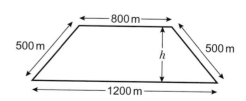

800 m
500 m   500 m
h
1200 m

> Form a triangle at the end of the trapezium and find its base and height. This will give the vertical height, h, of the trapezium.

CHECK Tick each box as your **confidence** in this topic improves.

Need extra help? Go to pages 66 and 67 and tick the boxes next to Q6, 7, 8 and 9. Then have a go at them once you've finished 7.1–7.5.

1 The diagram shows a cuboid.

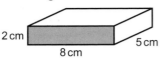

2 cm
8 cm
5 cm

$V = l \times w \times h$
Which part of the formula gives the area of the cross-section?

A right prism is a solid shape that has the same cross-section throughout its length.
The cross-section can be any flat shape. It is at right angles to the length of the solid.

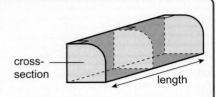

cross-section
length

a Work out the area of the shaded cross-section. ....

b Multiply the area of the cross-section by the length of the solid.

c What is the volume of the cuboid? ....

2 For each object work out
i its volume   **ii** its total surface area.
Give your answers to an appropriate degree of accuracy.

To find the surface area, sketch the net and work out the area of all the faces.

a

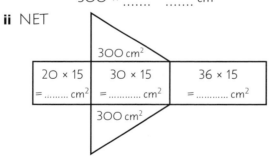

20 cm
36 cm
30 cm
15 cm

Sketch the cross-section.

20 cm
30 cm

i Area of cross-section = $\frac{1}{2}$ × base × height
= 0.5 × 20 × 30 = 300 cm²

Volume = area of cross-section × length
= 300 × .... = ... cm³

ii NET

300 cm²

| 20 × 15 = ... cm² | 30 × 15 = ... cm² | 36 × 15 = ... cm² |

300 cm²

Total surface area = 2 × 300 + ... + ... + ...
= .... cm²

b

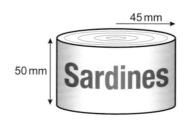

30 mm
8 mm
40 mm
10 mm

i Area of cross-section = $\frac{1}{2}(a + b) \times h$
= ....
= .... mm²

Volume = ... × .... = ... mm³

ii

3 a Work out the volume of this can of sardines. Give your answer to an appropriate degree of accuracy.

45 mm
50 mm
Sardines

Volume of a cylinder = $\pi r^2 h$

Literacy hint

A cylinder is a right prism with a circular cross-section.

b Work out the area of the label around the can by completing these statements.
Length of label = circumference of tin = π × 90 mm
Area of rectangular label = base × height = π × 90 mm × .... mm = ... mm²

CHECK   Tick each box as your **confidence** in this topic improves.

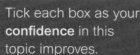

Need extra help? Go to page 67 and tick the boxes next to Q10 and 11. Then have a go at them once you've finished 7.1–7.5.

64

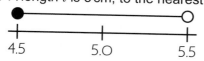
1 Draw an inequality to show the lower and upper bounds for each measurement.

  a A length l is 5 cm, to the nearest cm.

4.5	5.0	5.5

> The upper bound is 5.5 cm. The lower bound is 4.5 cm. $4.5 \leq l < 5.5$

  b A mass m is 9 kg, to the nearest kg.

  c A mass m is 20 kg, to the nearest 10 kg.

2 STEM / Problem-solving Chris makes cloth handbags from rectangular sheets of cloth.

  a The width of the cloth is 40 cm, to the nearest cm.
    What are the lower and upper bounds? ....

  b The length of the cloth is 70 cm to the nearest 10 cm.
    What are the lower and upper bounds? ....

  c Work out the lower and upper bounds for the area A of the cloth.
    Write your answer as an inequality, using 3 significant figures.

> Sketch and label the smallest and largest possible rectangles.

3 The mass m of a 500 g pack of lentils has a 5% error interval.
  Work out the minimum and maximum values for m.

> An error interval tells you the minimum and maximum possible measurement.

  5% of 500 g = 5 ÷ 100 × 500 = 25 g — [Work out 5% of 500.]

  Maximum mass = 500 + ... = ... g   Minimum mass = 500 − .... = ... g

  .... ≤ m < .... — [Write your answer as an inequality.]

4 STEM A machine fills 400 g pasta boxes with a ±2% error. One day it fills 50 000 boxes with the maximum amount possible. How much extra pasta (in grams) does it use than if it had been filling at the minimum?

5 STEM / Reasoning The diagram shows a circular shortbread biscuit.
  The measurements are to the nearest mm.
  A cardboard tube contains 20 biscuits stacked on top of each other.
  A 5 mm deep metal top is pushed into the tube.
  The bottom of the tube is cardboard.
  Work out the maximum total area of cardboard needed to make the tube.
  Give your answer to an appropriate degree of accuracy.

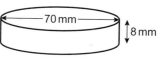

70 mm   8 mm

CHECK   Tick each box as your **confidence** in this topic improves.

Need extra help? Go to page 67 and tick the box next to Q12. Then have a go at it once you've finished 7.1–7.5.

65

7 Strengthen

Circles

1 Circumference, $C = \pi \times$ diameter

   a What is the diameter of this circle? ....

   b Work out the circumference. Give your answer to 1 decimal place.

     $C = \pi \times$ .... = ... cm

> Write down the calculation before you use your calculator.

2 Work out the circumference of this circle using the formula $C = \pi \times d$. Give your answer to 1 decimal place.

3 Area $= \pi \times$ radius^2

   a What is the radius of this circle? ....

   b Work out the area. Give your answer to 1 decimal place.

     $A = \pi \times$ ....^{2} = ... m^2

4 Work out the area of this circle.

> Work out the radius first.

> Use an inverse function machine.
> $A = \pi r^2$, so divide the area by π and take the square root to find the radius.

5 Work out the radius of a circle with an area of 50 cm^2. Give your answer to 1 decimal place.

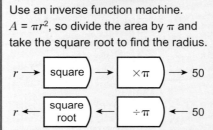

Pythagoras' theorem

6 On each triangle

   a label the hypotenuse of each triangle c

   b label the two shorter sides a and b.

> The hypotenuse is the longest side and is opposite the right angle. It doesn't matter which side length is a and which is b.

i 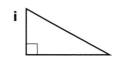   **ii**    **iii**

7 Use the formula $c^2 = a^2 + b^2$ to work out the length of the hypotenuse of each triangle. Give your answers to the nearest mm.

a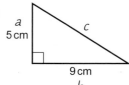

b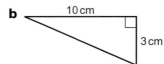

> Follow the same steps for triangle **b**.

$a = 5, b = 9$

$c^2 = a^2 + b^2$

$c^2 =$ ....$^2 +$ ....$^2 =$ ....

$c = \sqrt{...............} =$ ....

   $=$ .... (nearest mm)

8 Use the formula $c^2 = a^2 + b^2$ to find the unknown side of each triangle.
Give your answers to the nearest mm.

a
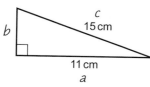

b

$c^2 = a^2 + b^2$

$15^2 = 11^2 + b^2$

$\text{.......} = \text{.......} + b^2$

$b^2 = \text{.......}$

$b = \sqrt{\text{.......}} = \text{.......}$

$= \text{.......}$ (nearest mm)

9 Problem-solving
Work out the area of this shape,
correct to 1 decimal place.

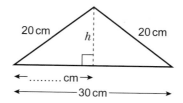

Use Pythagoras' theorem to work out the height first.

Prisms

10 a How many faces does this prism have? ....

b On a separate piece of paper sketch all the faces.
Label the measurements.

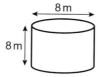

c Work out the area of each face.

Area of triangular face: $\frac{1}{2} \times 12 \times 5 = 30\,\text{cm}^2$ Area of top face: $10 \times 13 = \text{.......}$ cm²

d Work out the surface area of the prism.

$2 \times 30 + \text{..............................} = \text{...............}$ cm²

The surface area is the total area of all the faces. There are 2 triangular faces.

11 The diagram shows a cylinder.

a What is the radius? ....

b Work out the area of the cross-section, correct to 1 decimal place.

c Work out the volume of the cylinder, correct to 1 decimal place.

Measurements

12 A rectangle measures 80 cm by 30 cm, to the nearest 10 cm.

The smallest height and width will give the smallest rectangle

a Write the lower and upper bounds for the length, l. ....

b Write the lower and upper bounds for the width, w. ....

c Work out the area of the smallest possible rectangle. ....

d Work out the area of the largest possible rectangle. ....

e Complete the inequality for the area, A. .... cm² $\leq A <$ .... cm²

1 Work out the area and perimeter of this shape.

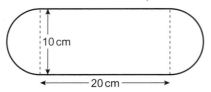

$$Area = \pi r^2 + b \times h$$ ───── The shape can be thought of as two semicircles and a rectangle.

2 Modelling The diagram shows a car tyre.

   a Work out the circumference of the wheel to the nearest cm.

←── 914 mm ──→

   b How far has the car travelled after 100 000 revolutions of the wheel?

   c How many times does the tyre turn in 2 km?

Worked example

3 Problem-solving / Real The diagram shows part of a metal strip.
The metal strip is 10 m long and 25 mm wide.
Holes are punched through the metal strip to make coins.
Each coin has a diameter of 18 mm.
The gap between each hole and the next is 2 mm.
The gap between the end of the strip and a hole is 9 mm.

9 mm

   a How many coins can be punched out of the metal strip?

   b Work out the area of metal strip left over.

4 Problem-solving The diagram shows a car tyre.
   a The circumference of the tyre is 396 cm. Work out its radius.

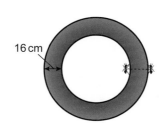
16 cm

Two ants are walking clockwise at the same speed around the tyre,
one around the outer edge, one around the inner edge.

   b The ants start walking at the dotted line. When the ant on the inner edge has completed one lap,
   how far does the ant on the outer edge still have to go to reach the dotted line?

5 Problem-solving Each square in the diagram has a side length 2 cm.
Work out the total length of all lines in the diagram.

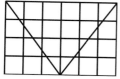

6 A line is drawn on a grid between the points (2, 2) and (4, 7).
Work out the length of the line, correct to 1 decimal place.

Strategy hint
Draw a diagram.

7 STEM / Modelling The tip of an F8F Bearcat airplane's
propeller travels at 2100 km/h.

a Convert 2100 km/h to m/s.

b Each propeller blade has a length of 2 m.
How long does it take for a blade to rotate 360°?
Give your answer to 3 decimal places.

> Compound measures like km/h are used
> to show how one quantity changes with
> another. Examples are
> • a speed of 25 km/h means 'every hour,
>   you travel 25 km'
> • the density of gold is 19.3 g/cm³ means
>   '1 cm³ of gold has a mass of 19.3 g'
> • a rate of flow of 5 l/min means 'every
>   1 minute, 5 l of liquid flows'.

8 STEM / Real A medium banana has a mass of approximately 102 g. A box of medium bananas
contains approximately 180 bananas. There is a ±20% error interval in the number of bananas and a
±5% error interval in the mass of a banana.
Work out the lower and upper bounds for the mass m of a box of medium bananas.

9 Modelling A gold coin has a diameter of 22.05 mm and is 1.52 mm thick.

a Work out the volume of the coin. Give your answer in cm³.

b The coin has a mass of 7.98 g. Work out the density of the coin.

10 Problem-solving The diagram shows a 75 cm tall container with a
quarter circle cross-section. The cross-section has a perimeter of 90 cm.

a Work out the radius of the container.

Water is poured into the container at a steady rate of 0.4 litres/second.

b How long does it take to fill the container?

75 cm

Write an equation
involving π and r.

7 Unit test

PROGRESS BAR Colour in the progress bar as you get questions correct.
Then fill in the progression chart on pages 104–108.

1 A circle has a diameter of 8.6 cm.

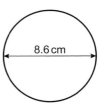

a Work out the radius of the circle. ....

b Work out the circumference of the circle.
Use a sensible degree of accuracy for your answer.

2 A circle has a circumference of 60 m. Give your answers to an appropriate degree of accuracy.
Work out

a the diameter **b** the radius **c** the area.

3 Calculate the length of the unknown side of each triangle.

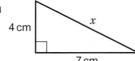

a

4 cm

x

7 cm

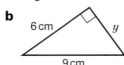

b

6 cm

y

9 cm

4 A box of matches contains 50 matches, to within a ±10% error interval.

a Work out the minimum and maximum possible number of matches in a box.

b Write the number of matches m in a box using an inequality.

5 a Work out the area of the cross-section of this prism.

b Work out the length of the sloping side, l.

c Work out the total surface area of the prism.

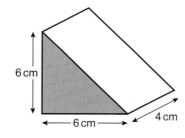

6 cm

6 cm

4 cm

6 A cylinder has a radius of 3 m and height of 8 m.

a Work out the volume of the cylinder, correct to the nearest m³.

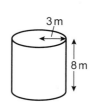

3 m

8 m

b Work out the total surface area of the cylinder, correct to the nearest m².

1 Complete these statements to generate the first three terms of the sequence $5n$.

When $n = 1$, $5n =$ ....

When $n = 2$, $5n =$ ....

When $n = 3$, $5n =$ ....

First three terms: ....

> To generate the 1st term, substitute $n = 1$ in the nth term.
> To generate the 2nd term, substitute $n = 2$ in the nth term.
> Write the terms in a list, separated by commas.

> **Literacy hint**
> 'To generate' means 'to create' or 'to produce'.

2 Write the first four terms of the sequence with nth term

a $2n$

b $2n + 3$

c $\frac{1}{2}n + 2$

d $10 - 3n$

> The nth term of a sequence is its position-to-term rule. It tells you how to work out the term at position n. The nth term is sometimes called the general term of the sequence.

Guided

3 Find the nth term of each sequence.

a 4, 9, 14, 19, ...

> The common difference is 5. Write out the first four terms of the sequence for $5n$, the multiples of 5. Compare the two sequences.

$5n$ 5, 10, 15, 20, ...

    4, 9, 14, 19, ... ⟩ -1

> Work out how to get from each term in $5n$ to each term in the sequence.

The nth term is ... $n - 1$

b 6, 8, 10, 12, ...

> To find the nth term of an arithmetic sequence:
> 1 Find the common difference.
> 2 If the common difference is 3, compare with the sequence for $3n$.
> 3 If the common difference is 4, compare with the sequence for $4n$, and so on

Worked example

c 35, 30, 25, 20, ...

> When the common difference is negative, compare with the multiples of a negative number.

4 Work out

  i the 10th term

  ii the 100th term of each sequence in Question 3.

a

  i ....

  ii ....

> To find the 10th term, substitute $n = 10$.

b

  i ....

  ii ....

c

  i ....

  ii ....

5 Here is a sequence of fractions. $\frac{1}{5}, \frac{4}{9}, \frac{7}{13}, \frac{10}{17}, \frac{13}{21}, \dots$

a Work out the nth term.

> Work out the nth term of the numerator and the nth term of the denominator.

b What do you look for in the terms of a sequence to help you find the nth term?

> **CHECK** Tick each box as your **confidence** in this topic improves.

> **Need extra help?** Go to page 79 and tick the boxes next to Q1, 2, 3 and 4. Then have a go at them once you've finished 8.1–8.8.

8.2 Non-linear sequences

1 All these sequences are geometric sequences.

For each one, write the term-to-term rule 'multiply by ...' and find the next term.

> In a geometric sequence, the term-to-term rule is 'multiply by a number'.

a 1, 2, 4, 8, ...

$\times 2 \quad \times 2 \quad \times 2$

1   2   4   8   multiply by .... next term ....

b 1, 10, 100, 1000, ...   multiply by .... next term ....

c 640, 160, 40, 10, ...   multiply by .... next term ....

2 Problem-solving For this geometric sequence, find the first term that is less than 1.

5000, 1000, 200, ...

3 Work out the term-to-term rule for each sequence and write down the next two terms.

$\times -2 \quad \times -2 \quad \times -2$

a 2, –4, 8, –16, ...   2   –4   8   –16   rule is ...., next two terms are ...., ...

b –5, 50, –500, 5000, ...

4 Modelling / Problem-solving Each hour a lab technician records the number of bacteria on a piece of warm, raw chicken.

Time (hours)	1	2	3
Number of bacteria	5	40	320

She says, 'If the bacteria continue to grow in the same way, there will be over a million bacteria in just 4 more hours!' Is she correct? Explain.

5 Write down the first five terms of the sequence with nth term

a n^2 ....

b $n^2 + 10$ ....

6 Here is the sequence $n^2 + 3$.

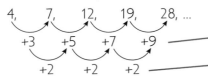

4,   7,   12,   19,   28, ...

+3   +5   +7   +9   → 1st differences: the differences between terms

+2   +2   +2   → 2nd differences: the differences between 1st differences

a What is the pattern in the 1st differences? ....

b Use the pattern to work out the next term. ....

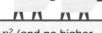

7 Sequences A and B, with nth terms below, are quadratic.

> An nth term that includes n^2 (and no higher power of n) generates a quadratic sequence.

a For both, write down

   i the first four terms

   ii the 1st differences   **iii** the 2nd differences.

     A $n^2 + 4$ B $n^2 - 2$

     i ....   **i** ....

     ii ....   **ii** ....

     iii ....   **iii** ....

b What do you notice about the 2nd differences of sequences with n^2 in the nth term? ....

CHECK Tick each box as your **confidence** in this topic improves.

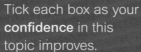

Need extra help? Go to page 79 and tick the box next to Q5. Then have a go at it once you've finished 8.1–8.8.

1 The distance–time graph shows a car journey.

Guided

a Between which times did the car travel fastest? How do you know?

Between .... am and .... am.

This is the steepest part of the graph.

b What was the average speed for the whole journey?

Total distance = ...

Total time = ...

> Read the total distance and total time from the graph.

Average speed = $\frac{\text{total distance}}{\text{total time}}$ = $\frac{.........}{.........}$ = ...

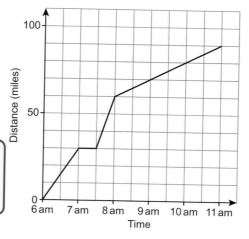

Worked example

A rate of change graph shows how a quantity changes over time. A distance–time graph is a rate of change graph because it shows how the distance travelled changes over time.

2 Real / Modelling Car A travels from Exeter to Cardiff. Car B travels from Cardiff to Exeter.

a Use the graph to work out how far they are from Cardiff when they pass each other.

b Which car travelled faster on average?

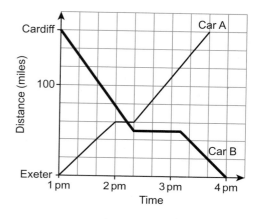

3 Real / Modelling A 1p coin is dropped from the top of a 200 m tall building. The table shows the coin's height above the ground for some of its fall.

Time, t (seconds)	1	2	3	4	5
Height, h (m)	196	188	177	164	150

a Draw a graph to show this information.

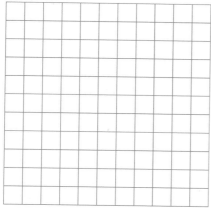

> Put 'Time' on the horizontal axis and 'Height' on the vertical axis.
> Plot the points and join them with a smooth curve.
> Your vertical axis could start at 150 m and finish at 200 m.

b Is the coin travelling at constant speed? How can you tell? ....

CHECK   Tick each box as your **confidence** in this topic improves.   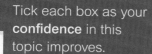

 Need extra help? Go to page 80 and tick the box next to Q6. Then have a go at it once you've finished 8.1–8.8.

8.4 Using $y = mx + c$

1 Here are the equations of two lines.

$y = 4x$ $\qquad\qquad$ $y = \frac{1}{4}x$

Which is steeper? How can you tell? ....

2 Draw these graphs from their equations.

  a $y = 2x + 1$

  b $y = x - 3$

  c $y = -x - 1$

  d $y = -3x - 3$

  e $y = \frac{1}{2}x - 4$

  f $y = -\frac{1}{2}x - 2$

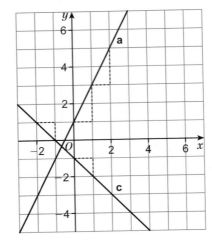

Plot the y-intercept.
Decide if the gradient
is positive or negative.
Draw a line with this
gradient, starting from
the y-intercept.
Extend your line right
across the grid.
Label the line.

3 Without drawing the graphs, sort these equations into pairs of parallel lines.

  A $y = 3x + 3$ $\qquad$ B $y = \frac{1}{4}x + 1$ $\qquad$ C $y = 2x$

  D $y = 0.25x - 3$ $\qquad$ E $y = 3x - 1.5$ $\qquad$ F $y = 2x - 8$

What do you know
about the gradients
of parallel lines?

4 Write the equation of the line parallel to

  a $y = 2x + 3$ with y-intercept $(0, -4)$

  b $y = \frac{1}{2}x - 2$ with y-intercept $(0, 7)$

5 a What is the x-coordinate of every point on the line $x = 5$? ....

  b Where does the line $y = 2x + 3$ cross the line $x = 5$?

Strategy hint

Substitute your x-value from
part **a** into the equation of
the line to get the y-value.
Write the x- and y-values as
coordinates.

6 Problem-solving In a video game, a character
moves along the line $y = 3x + 2$.
A mountain bike is at the point $(2, 7)$.

What is the x-coordinate at the point $(2, 7)$?
Substitute this into the equation of the line.
Does it give the correct y-value?

  a Will the character get to the mountain bike? ....

The character continues to move along the same line in search of other rewards.

  b Tick which of these rewards it will get to.

  football at $(-2, -4)$ ☐ $\qquad$ hockey stick at $(-3, -6)$ ☐ $\qquad$ inline skates at $(-3.5, 0)$ ☐

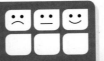

CHECK Tick each box as your
confidence in this
topic improves.

Need extra help? Go to page 80 and tick
the boxes next to Q7 and 8. Then have a
go at them once you've finished 8.1–8.8.

8.5 More straight-line graphs

1 a What is the value of x at any point on the y-axis? ....

b What is the value of y at any point on the x-axis? ....

c Complete.

   i The y-intercept of a graph has x-coordinate ....

   ii The x-intercept of a graph has y-coordinate ....

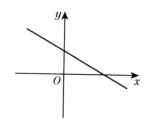

2 Plot and label the graph of $3x + 2y = 9$.

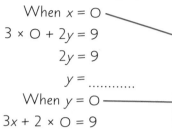

When $x = 0$

$3 \times 0 + 2y = 9$

$2y = 9$

$y = $ ....

> To find the y-intercept, substitute $x = 0$ into the equation.
> Solve to find the value of y.

When $y = 0$

$3x + 2 \times 0 = 9$

$3x = 9$

$x = $ ....

> To find the x-intercept, substitute $y = 0$ into the equation.
> Solve to find the value of x.

x	0	
y		0

> Draw a table of values with $x = 0$ and $y = 0$.

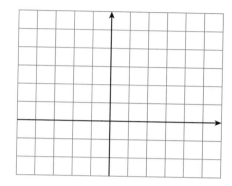

3 On the grid in Question 2, plot and label the graph of $2x - y = -5$.

Worked example

4 Which is the steepest line?

   A $y = 3x - 2$ B $8x + 4y = 6$ C $5x - y = 12$

> To compare the gradients of two straight lines, their equations need to be in the form $y = mx + c$.
> Make y the subject. Write the x-term first on the right-hand side.

5 Which of these lines pass through $(0, -4)$? Show how you worked it out.

   A $y = -4x + 2$ B $y = 2x - 4$ C $5x + 2y = -8$ D $3x + y = 4$

6 a i Write the equation $y = 2x + 5$ using a function machine.

$x \longrightarrow \boxed{\times 2} \longrightarrow \boxed{+5} \longrightarrow y$

   ii Work out the inverse function of $y = 2x + 5$ using a function machine.

$x \longleftarrow \boxed{......} \longleftarrow \boxed{......} \longleftarrow y$ $x = \dfrac{y................}{................}$

b Write the inverse function of $y = 3x - 4$.

CHECK Tick each box as your **confidence** in this topic improves.

Need extra help? Go to page 81 and tick the box next to Q10. Then have a go at it once you've finished 8.1–8.8.

8.6 More simultaneous equations

1 Draw graphs to solve these simultaneous equations.
Write down the point of intersection.

a $4x - y = 3$ $(0, \text{.......})$ and $(\frac{3}{4}, 0)$

    $2x - y = -1$ $(0, 1)$ and $(\text{.......}, 0)$

    Intersection point: ....

    Solution: $x = \text{...........}, y = \text{...........}$

b $y + 2x = -2$

    $2y - x = 3$

    Intersection point: ....

    Solution: $x = \text{...........}, y = \text{...........}$

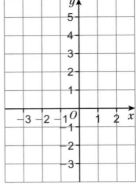

> The point where two (or more) lines cross is called the point of intersection.

> You can find the solution to a pair of simultaneous equations by
> 1 drawing the lines on a coordinate grid
> 2 finding the point of intersection.

2 Real / Modelling Amy bought 4 cups of tea and 3 cakes for £6.00.
Ben bought 2 cups of tea and 4 cakes for £5.50.

    a Write equations for Amy and Ben.

    b Solve your simultaneous equations graphically.

    c What is the cost of a cake? ....

> Use x for the cost of a cup of tea.

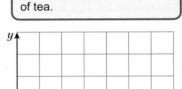

3 Find the equation of the line that passes through

    a the points A(1, 7) and B(3, 11)

At A, $x = 1$ and $y = 7$.

Substituting into $y = mx + c$:

       $7 = m \times 1 + c$

       $7 = m + c$

At B, $x = 3$ and $y = 11$.

Substituting into $y = mx + c$:

       $11 = m \times 3 + c$

       $11 = 3m + c$

> The points lie on the line, so their coordinates 'fit' the equation for the line. Use the x- and y-values from each coordinate pair to write an equation for the line using $y = mx + c$.

$7 = m + c$ ①

$11 = 3m + c$ ②

$4 = 2m$ ② − ①

$2 = m$

Substitute $m = 2$ into equation ①.

$7 = 2 + c$

$c = 5$

Equation of line is $y = 2x + 5$.

> Solve the simultaneous equations to find m and c.

> Substitute the values of m and c into $y = mx + c$.

    b the points P(2, 7) and Q(−2, −5).

CHECK Tick each box as your **confidence** in this topic improves.

Need extra help? Go to page 80 and tick the box next to Q9. Then have a go at it once you've finished 8.1–8.8.

Guided

1 a Complete this table of values for $y = x^2$.

x	−4	−3	−2	−1	0	1	2	3	4
$y = x^2$	16				O	1	4		

A quadratic equation contains a term in x^2 but no higher power of x. The graph of a quadratic equation is a curved shape called a parabola.

b Plot the graph of $y = x^2$.
Label your graph with its equation.

c Complete the table above for values for $y = 2x^2$.

d Plot the graph of $y = 2x^2$.
Plot using the x-axis from −3 to 3.
Label your graph with its equation.

e What do you notice is the same of the graphs for $y = x^2$ and $y = 2x^2$?

f Describe the symmetry of each graph by giving the equation of its mirror line.

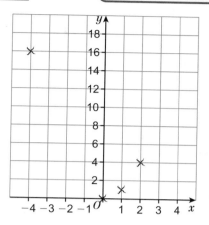

Worked example

2 a Complete this table of values for $y = x^2 + 1$.

x	−3	−2	−1	0	1	2	3
x^2							
+ 1	+ 1	+ 1	+ 1	+ 1	+ 1	+ 1	+ 1
y							

For quadratic functions with more than one step, you can include a row for each step in the table.

b Plot and label the graph of $y = x^2 + 1$ on the grid in Question 1.

c Plot and label the graph of $y = x^2 + 2$ on the grid in Question 1.

3 Modelling / STEM A scientist is studying the effect of air resistance on spheres.
She drops two spheres of equal mass, but different air resistance. The data shows the distance fallen each second by the two spheres dropped from the top of a tower.

Sphere 1

Time (s)	1	2	3	4	5
Distance (m)	3	12	27	48	75

Sphere 2

Time (s)	1	2	3	4	5
Distance (m)	4	16	36	64	100

a Plot the graphs for both sets of data.

b What type of graph do you think these are?

c **Reasoning** Which graph shows the sphere with the greater air resistance?
Label the graph A.
Explain your answer.

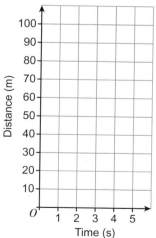

d When is sphere A falling fastest? ....

CHECK Tick each box as your **confidence** in this topic improves.

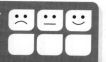

Need extra help? Go to page 81 and tick the box next to Q11. Then have a go at it once you've finished 8.1–8.8.

77

8.8 Non-linear graphs

1 a Complete this table of values for $y = x^3$.

> A cubic equation contains a term in x^3 but no higher power of x.

x	−4	−3	−2	−1	0	1	2	3	4
$y = x^3$	−64				$\bigcirc$	1	8		

b Plot the graph of $y = x^3$. Join the points with a smooth curve. Label your graph with its equation.

c Use your graph to estimate

   i 2.5^3 ....   **ii** $\sqrt[3]{50}$ ....

d Complete the table above for values for $y = 2x^3$.

e Plot the graph of $y = 2x^3$. Plot using the x-axis from −3 to 3. Label your graph with its equation.

f What is the same about your two graphs? What is different?

Worked example

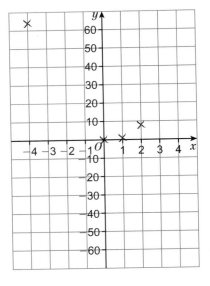

2 Real / STEM The table gives the volumes of four bird baths with different sizes of radius.

Radius, r (cm)	5	6	7	8	9
Volume, V (cm³)	80	140	230	335	445

a Plot a graph for these values.

b Use your graph to estimate the volume of a bird bath with radius 8.5 cm. ....

c Use your graph to estimate the radius of a bird bath with a volume of 200 cm³. ....

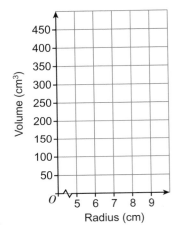

3 Modelling / Finance Ishmael borrowed £5000 from his mother. He pays back the same small percentage of the remaining debt every month.
The graph shows how much he owes his mother.

a How much does he pay back in the first year?

b What percentage of the £5000 does he still owe at the start of the second year?

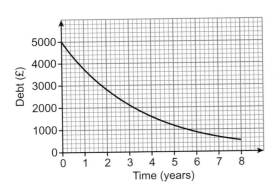

c How much does he owe after 2 years? ....

d How long does it take him to reduce his debt to £1000? ....

CHECK   Tick each box as your **confidence** in this topic improves.

Need extra help? Go to page 81 and tick the box next to Q12. Then have a go at it once you've finished 8.1–8.8.

Sequences

1 In this table, n gives the number of the term.

a Complete the table of values for the sequence with nth term $3n$.

n	1	2	3	4	5
$3n$	3	6			
$3n - 2$	1				

> The n-value gives the position: $n = 1$ is the 1st term, $n = 2$ is the 2nd term, and so on.
> In part **b**, substitute
> • $n = 1$ to find the 1st term: $3 \times 1 - 2$
> • $n = 2$ to find the 2nd term: $3 \times 2 - 2$, and so on.

b Write down the first five terms of the sequence $3n - 2$.

2 Work out the first five terms of the sequences with these nth terms.

a $3n + 3$

b $5n + 2$

> You could draw a table of values like the one in Q1.

c $\frac{1}{2}n + 1$

d $20 - 2n$

3 Complete this table to work out the nth term of the sequence 7, 10, 13, 16, ...

Sequence		7	10	13	16
Differences			+3	+.....	+.....
Multiples of 3 ($3n$)		3	6		

nth term is ....

> **1** Work out and write the differences between terms.
> **2** Write out the first four multiples of the difference.
> How do you get from the multiples to the terms in the sequence?
> **3** Check your nth term. Substitute $n = 1$. Do you get 7 (the first term)?

4 Work out the nth term of each sequence.

a 9, 14, 19, 24, ...

b 1, 3, 5, 7, ...

c 13, 11, 9, 7, ...

> Draw a table for each sequence, like the one in Q3.

Worked example

5 Reasoning

a Tess thinks that the sequence 50, 47, 44, 41, 38, ... is an arithmetic sequence.
Is she correct? Explain how you know.

> In an arithmetic sequence you add or subtract the same amount to get from one term to the next.

b Tess thinks that the sequence 50, 49, 47, 44, 40, ... is a geometric sequence.
Is she correct? Explain how you know.

> In a geometric sequence, the term-to-term rule is 'multiply by a number'.

Straight-line graphs

6 Gill left her house at 1 pm. She walked 4 miles in $1\frac{1}{2}$ hours. Then she rested for half an hour before she walked back. She arrived home at 5 pm.

   a Draw a graph to show this information.

   b What speed was she walking on her walk back?

   c What was Gill's average speed for the whole journey?

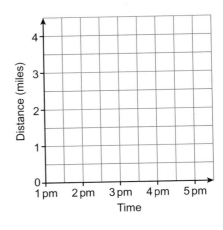

Guided

7 a Complete the table.

   b Write down the equations of the lines that are parallel.

   c Write down the equations of the lines that have the same y-intercept.

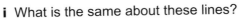

$y = mx + c$	Gradient m	y-intercept $(0, c)$
$y = 2x + 6$	2	$(0, 6)$
$y = -4x + 1$		
$y = 2x + 1$		
$y = \frac{1}{4}x - 7$		

   d Which line slopes in the opposite direction to the others?

> Parallel lines have the same _____
> Positive gradients slope uphill left to right.
> Negative gradients slope downhill left to right.

8 a Reasoning

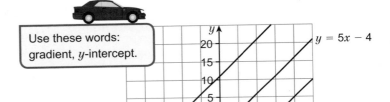

Use these words: gradient, y-intercept.

   i What is the same about these lines?

   ii What is different about them?

   b Circle the equations which give lines parallel to $y = 5x - 4$.

     A $y = 5x - 0.5$ B $y = \frac{1}{5}x + 2$

     C $y = 2.5x - 2.5$ D $y = 5x + 246$

$y = 5x - 4$

9 a Find the point where the line $8x + 4y = 12$

     i crosses the y-axis   **ii** crosses the x-axis.

> The line crosses the y-axis at $(0, \square)$.
> For each point, substitute the value you know into the equation.

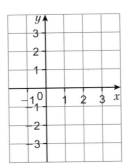

   b Plot the points you found in part **a**, and join them with a straight line.

   c Plot the graph of $6x - 2y = 4$.

   d Write down the point of intersection of these simultaneous equations. ....

10 a Complete these function machines to rearrange $9x + 3y = 15$ into the form $y = mx + c$.

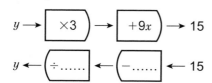

$y \rightarrow \boxed{\times 3} \rightarrow \boxed{+9x} \rightarrow 15$

$y \leftarrow \boxed{\div \dots} \leftarrow \boxed{- \dots} \leftarrow 15$

> Start with y.
> What do you do to y to get the number on the right-hand side? Then go back the other way, starting with 15.
> $$y = \frac{15 - \square}{3} = \frac{15}{3} - \frac{\square}{3}$$
> $$y = \square + \square$$
> For the last step, write in the x term first, then the number term, in the form $y = mx + c$.

b Use the similar steps to write each equation in the form $y = mx + c$.

i $4x + 12y = 8$ **ii** $-2x + 6y = -2$

Non-linear graphs

11 Problem-solving Match each equation to one of the graphs below.

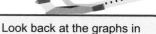

> Look back at the graphs in 8.4, 8.7 and 8.8 to help you.

i $y = x^2 + 5$ ....   **ii** $y = 2x + 5$ ....

iii $y = -x^2 + 5$ ....   **iv** $y = -2x + 5$ ....

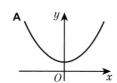 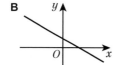 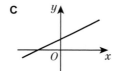 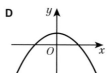

12 Modelling The graph shows the growth of one of Greg's tomato plants.

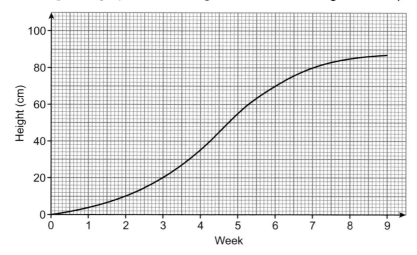

a How tall is the plant at week 4? ....

b When does the plant reach 80 cm? ....

c At week 10, the average height of Greg's five tomato plants is 93 cm.
Do you think the size of this tomato plant is taller or shorter than average? Explain.

1 Problem-solving Write the next three terms in this sequence.

2, 2, 3, 5, 8, 12, 17, 23, ...

2 Problem-solving / Modelling Here is a pattern of grey and white tiles.

  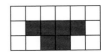

a Complete this table for the sequences of the numbers of white tiles and the numbers of grey tiles.

Pattern number	1	2	3	4	5
Number of white tiles	10	11			
Number of grey tiles	2	4			

b Write down the nth term for the sequence of grey tiles.

c Write down the nth term for the sequence of white tiles.

d How many grey tiles will there be in the 10th pattern?

e How many white tiles will there be in the 100th pattern?

f Kev has 50 white tiles and 100 grey tiles.
Which is the largest complete pattern he can make?

> Use the nth term.

> **Literacy hint**
> When a region satisfies an inequality, all the points in it 'fit' the inequality.

3 On a coordinate grid, show the region given by the inequalities.
Show clearly the region given by each pair of inequalities.

a $x \leqslant 3, y > -2$

b $x > 3, y \leqslant 4$

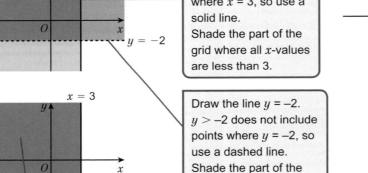

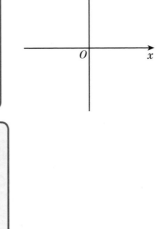

> Draw the line $x = 3$.
> $x \leqslant 3$ includes points where $x = 3$, so use a solid line.
> Shade the part of the grid where all x-values are less than 3.

> Draw the line $y = -2$.
> $y > -2$ does not include points where $y = -2$, so use a dashed line.
> Shade the part of the grid where all y-values are greater than -2.

> The region that satisfies both inequalities is where all points have x-coordinate $\leqslant 3$ and y-coordinate > -2.
> This is where the regions for the two inequalities overlap.

4 Problem-solving

a Draw graphs to show the regions satisfied by $x < 2, y \leqslant 2x + 1$.

b Show clearly the region satisfied by both inequalities.

> Choose any point in the region that satisfies both inequalities.
> Write the x and y values at that point.

c Write a pair of positive x- and y-values that satisfy both inequalities simultaneously.

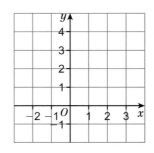

d Write a pair of negative x- and y-values that satisfy both inequalities simultaneously.

5 Problem-solving Here are the first four terms of some sequences.

a What are the 2nd differences of the sequences with n^2 in the nth term?

b What are the 2nd differences of the sequences with $2n^2$ in the nth term?

c Work out the 2nd differences of this sequence: 5, 11, 21, 35, …

n^2	1, 4, 9, 16
$n^2 - 1$	0, 3, 8, 15
$n^2 + 3$	4, 7, 12, 19
$2n^2$	2, 8, 18, 32
$2n^2 + 1$	3, 9, 19, 33
$2n^2 - 4$	−2, 4, 14, 28

d Write down the term involving n^2 for the sequence in part **c**.

> Use your answers to parts **a** and **b**. Is it n^2 or $2n^2$?

e Work out the general term for the sequence 5, 11, 21, 35, …

6 Reasoning Match each equation to one of the graphs below.

i $y = x^2 + 3$ ....

ii $y = -x^2 + 3$ ....

iii $y = x^3$ ....

iv $y = -x^3 - 2$ ....

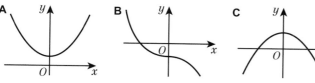
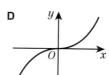

7 Real / Modelling The graph shows the number of adults (16+) who used the internet at least once a week in the UK.

a How many adults used the internet at least once a week in 2007? ....

b Between which 2 years was there the greatest increase in internet users?

c In which year did the number of adults using the internet at least once a week reach 35 million? ....

d How accurate do you think your answer to part **c** is? ....

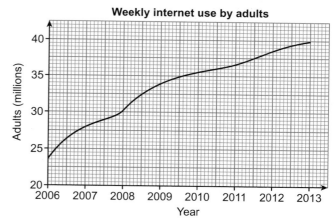

Weekly internet use by adults

Source: Office for National Statistics

e 23.6 million adults used the internet at least once a week in 2006.
How many more adults used the internet at least once a week in 2007? ....

f Work out the percentage increase in users from 2006 to 2013.

g Sian says, 'The graph cannot carry on increasing forever.' Sian is correct. Explain why.

8 Unit test

PROGRESS BAR Colour in the progress bar as you get questions correct. Then fill in the progression chart on pages 104–108.

1 Work out the nth term of the sequence 7, 16, 25, 34, …

2 Write down the first three terms of the sequences with nth term

    a $5n + 1$ ....   **b** $10 - 2n$ ....   **c** $n^2 + 3$ ....

3 Which of these equations give parallel lines? ....

    A $y = 2x + 3$ B $5y - 10x = 1$ C $6y + 12x = 6$ D $y = 2x - 2$

4 These patterns are made from black and white counters.

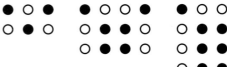

    a Complete the table.

Pattern number	1	2	3	4	5
White counters					
Black counters					

        1   2   3

    b Work out the nth term for the sequence of white counters. ....

    c Is the sequence of white counters an arithmetic sequence or a geometric sequence? Explain how you know.

    d Find the nth term of the sequence of black counters. ....

5 The graph shows the value of Claire's investment.

    a Estimate the value of Claire's investment in 2009.

    b Between which 2 years does her investment grow fastest? ....

    c When is Claire's investment worth £13 000?

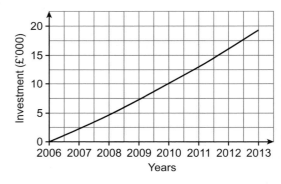

6 Write down the two inequalities that describe the shaded region.

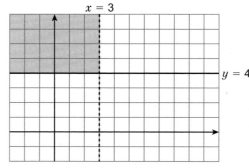

7 a On the same axes used in Question 6, draw the graph of $2x - y = 1$.

    b Use your graph to solve the simultaneous equations $2x - y = 1$ and $y = 4$.

8 Match each equation to one of the graphs.

    i $y = x^3 + 2$ ....   A   B   C   D

    ii $y = -x^3 + 2$ ....

    iii $y = x^2 + 2$ ....

    iv $y = 2x + 2$ ....

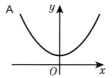 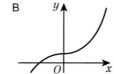 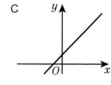

1 The table shows some information about Year 9 students.

	Pets	No pets	Total
Female	152	60	212
Male	147	41	188
Total	299	101	400

> **Literacy hint**
> 'Picked at random' means that each student is equally likely to be picked.

A student is picked at random. What is the probability that this student

a is female $\dfrac{\text{total number of females}}{\text{total number of students}} = \dfrac{..........}{400} = ...$

b does not have a pet ....

> $\dfrac{\text{total number of males}}{\text{total number of students}}$

c is a male who has pets? ....

d A teacher is talking to a Year 9 student who has a pet.
Is the teacher more likely to be talking to a male or a female student?
Explain your answer.

> Work out the totals and compare the probabilities.

2 Those attending a Year 9 parents' evening were asked to vote for the best piece of Year 9 art. The table shows the results.

	Painting	Ceramic	Mural	Total
Y9 boys	23	22	81	126
Y9 girls	41	25	67	133
Parents	124	93	44	261
Total	188	140	192	520

a A vote is picked at random.
What is the probability that the vote is from

   i a Year 9 boy who voted for the painting ....

   ii a parent who voted for the ceramic? ....

b A vote is picked at random. Which is more likely: a Year 9 girl who voted for the ceramic or a parent who voted for the ceramic? Show your working.

The art teacher picked a parent at random.
c What is the probability that this parent voted for the mural? ....

3 Modelling A bag contains red, white and blue balls. A ball is picked at random.
The table shows the probability of each colour.

Colour	red	white	blue
Probability	0.3	0.5	

> Events are mutually exclusive if one or other can happen, but not both at the same time. The probabilities of all the mutually exclusive outcomes of an event add to 1.

a Work out the probability that a blue ball is picked.
$0.3 + 0.5 = 0.8.$ $1 - 0.8 = 0.2$

> The colours in the table are the only three colours possible. They are mutually exclusive, so their probabilities must add up to 1.

b There are 30 balls in the bag.
How many are red? $0.3 \times .... = ...$

10 more balls are added to the bag. The table shows the new probabilities of each colour.

Colour	red	white	blue
Probability	0.25		0.35

c Problem-solving How many of the balls are white?

CHECK Tick each box as your **confidence** in this topic improves.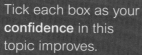

Need extra help? Go to pages 89 and 90 and tick the boxes next to Q1 and 4. Then have a go at them once you've finished 9.1–9.4.

85

9.2 Experimental probability

1 Modelling The table shows the results of an experiment spinning a 4-sided spinner.

Score	1	2	3	4
Frequency	23	24	28	25

> You can estimate the probability of an event from the results of an experiment or survey.
> $$\text{estimated probability} = \frac{\text{frequency of event}}{\text{total frequency}}$$
> This estimated probability is also known as experimental probability.

a How many times in total was the spinner spun?

23 + 24 + 28 + 25 = ...

b What is the estimated probability of spinning a 2? $\dfrac{24}{...........}$ = 0. ....

> 'P(event A)' is a short way of saying 'the probability of event A happening'.

c How many 3s would you expect in 1000 spins?   P(3) × 1000 = ...

2 Modelling Jason rolled two 4-sided dice 60 times and added up the numbers each time. He got a total of 5 on 16 occasions.

a Use a calculator to decide whether $\frac{1}{3}$, $\frac{1}{4}$ or $\frac{1}{5}$ is the best estimate for the probability of rolling a total of 5.

b Imagine Jason rolled the dice 320 times. Use your estimate to predict how many times he would get a total of 5.

3 Silvia's mother always gives her a serving of fruit with her pudding.
P(orange) = 0.1   P(apple) = 0.15   P(pineapple) = 0.3
P(pear) = 0.2   P(plum) = 0.1   P(peach) = 0.15
What is the probability that these are served with any one pudding?

> For two mutually exclusive events, you work out the probability that one or the other happens by adding together their probabilities.

a Pear or plum   ....

> Pear and plum are mutually exclusive. So P(pear or plum) = P(pear) + P(plum)

b Any fruit other than pear or plum   ....

4 Modelling A traffic surveyor records the day of the week and the time of crossing of cars at a toll bridge, over a 4-week period.

	00 00–05 59	06 00–11 59	12 00–17 59	18 00–23 59	Total
Weekday	19 256	82 044	77 772	42 152	221 224
Weekend	3216	5752	19 376	11 064	39 408
Total	22 472	87 796	97 148	53 216	260 632

a Use the data to work out the mean number of cars crossing
  i per day on the weekend

> Mean number of cars crossing each day at the weekend
> $$= \frac{\text{total number of cars crossing in one weekend}}{\text{number of days in a weekend}}$$

  ii on a weekday.

b Are cars more likely to be crossing the bridge at the weekend or on a weekday? Explain your answer.

c It is expected that 12 000 cars will cross the bridge the following week. How many will be expected to cross between 06 00 and 11 59? Show your working.

CHECK   Tick each box as your **confidence** in this topic improves.

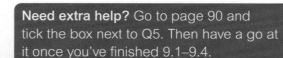

Need extra help? Go to page 90 and tick the box next to Q5. Then have a go at it once you've finished 9.1–9.4.

1 24 students have dogs as pets and 10 have cats. 6 students have both.

a Show this information in a Venn diagram.

A Venn diagram shows sets of data in circles inside a rectangle. You write data that is in both sets in the part where the circles overlap.

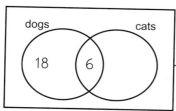

Draw two overlapping circles, one for each set of data. 6 students have dogs and cats, so put 6 in the overlap

$24 - 6 = 18$

$10 - \text{......} = \text{......}$

Work out how many are left in the rest of each set and write the values in. 24 students have dogs, but 6 of these also have cats. So 18 have only dogs.

b What is the probability that a student picked at random

   i has dogs $\dfrac{\text{number of students with dogs}}{\text{total number of students}} = \dfrac{\text{............}}{18 + 6 + 4} = \text{.......}$

   ii has dogs but not cats? ....

24 students have dogs.

Look at the Venn diagram above left. Which value gives the number of students who only have dogs?

2 The Venn diagram shows students' snacks of crisps (C), sandwiches (S) or muesli bars (M).

   a How many students had crisps, sandwiches and a muesli bar?

   b How many students had crisps and sandwiches but not a muesli bar?

   c What is the probability that one of these students, picked at random, had a muesli bar?

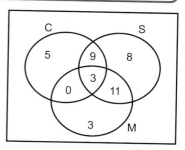

How many students were asked altogether?

3 Modelling Jon and Fay roll one 4-sided dice and one 6-sided dice.

   a Complete this sample space diagram to show all the possible outcomes.

   b How many equally likely outcomes are there?

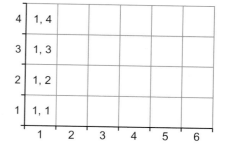

The scores of each dice are added to give a total.
If the total is 6 or more, Fay wins. Jon says it isn't fair.

   c Explain why it isn't fair.

Include the probability of Fay winning.

Worked example

   d If the game were played 60 times, how many times would you expect Fay to win?

   e How could the rules be changed to make it fair?

4 Problem-solving / Modelling Every week all the players in a bingo competition are entered into a prize draw. There is one prize draw for the men and one for the women. Explain why this might not give everyone a fair chance of winning.

CHECK Tick each box as your **confidence** in this topic improves.

Need extra help? Go to pages 89 and 90 and tick the boxes next to Q2 and 3. Then have a go at them once you've finished 9.1–9.4.

9.4 Independent events

1 In a bag there are 3 red and 2 orange sweets.

a What is the probability of picking a red sweet? ....

Gary picks a sweet at random. It's red, and he eats it.
Gary picks another sweet at random.

b What is the probability that he picks a red sweet this time? ....

2 Which of these pairs of events are independent? ....

   A Flipping a coin getting 'heads', then flipping it again, getting 'tails'

   B Picking a vanilla yogurt, eating it, then picking another yogurt

   C Picking an ace from a pack of cards, and then picking another ace

   D Choosing the winning horse in a race, then choosing the winning horse in the next race

> Two events are independent if the result of one does not affect the result of another.

3 There are 3 £1 and 4 €1 coins in a bag.
Tania picks a coin, replaces it, and picks again.

> A tree diagram helps you work out the combined probabilities of more than one event.

a Draw a tree diagram to show the possible outcomes.

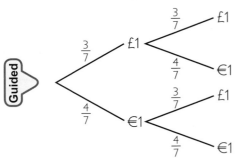

> At each pick the choice is £1 or €1. Draw a branch for £1 and one for €1 each time. Write the P(£) value on each branch for £1 and the P(€) value on each branch for €1.

> The probability of two independent events is P(event 1) × P(event 2)

> Read along the branches for £1, £1.
> Multiply the probabilities P(£) × P(£) = P(£,£)

b Work out the probability that she picks 2 £1 coins. $P(£, £) = \frac{3}{7} \times \frac{3}{7} =$ ....

c Work out the probability that she picks one £1 and one €1.

one £1 and one €1 could be P(£, €) or P(€, £)

$P(£, €) = \frac{3}{7} \times \frac{4}{7} =$ .... $P(€, £) =$ ....

$P(£, €) + P(€, £) =$ .... + ... = ...

> Find all the paths through the diagram that give one £1 and one €1.

4 Real / Modelling Jun is learning to ride a skateboard. She predicts the chance of doing a stunt called a fakie is 0.6 on her first try and 0.7 on her second try.

a Draw a tree diagram to show the possible outcomes of her first two tries.

> **Worked example**
>
>

b What is the probability that Jun succeeds with both her attempts at a fakie? ....

CHECK Tick each box as your **confidence** in this topic improves.

Need extra help? Go to page 90 and tick the boxes next to Q5 and 6. Then have a go at them once you've finished 9.1–9.4.

88

Probability from tables and diagrams

1 The table shows data on numbers of toys made on two production lines.

	Mon	Tue	Wed	Thu	Fri	Total
Line A (× 1000)	7.2	7.3	7.2	7.1	6.9	35.7
Line B (× 1000)	4.7	6.8	7.4	7.4	7.4	33.7
Total (× 1000)	11.9	14.1	14.6	14.5	14.3	69.4

a How many toys did line A produce from Monday to Wednesday?

7200 + 7300 + 7200 = 21700

b What is the probability that a toy picked at random was produced on line A from Monday to Wednesday?

> Use your answer to part **a** and the total number of toys produced.

c A toy from line B is picked at random. What is the probability that it was produced on Monday or Tuesday?

> Use only the values for line B.

2 Modelling Jodi and Rick each have a bag containing shapes. Jodi's bag has a square and a circle. Rick's bag has a square, a circle and a triangle.
A shape is picked at random from each bag.

a Complete the sample space diagram to show all the possible outcomes.

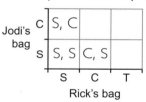

> S = square, C = circle and T = triangle

b How many possible outcomes are there? ....

c What is the probability that the two shapes are both circles?

d What is the probability of getting at least one square?

> **Literacy hint**
> 'At least one square' means one or more squares.

Jodi and Rick each add a hexagon to their bags.

e Draw a new sample space diagram to show the possible outcomes when picking a shape at random from each bag.

A shape is picked at random from each bag.

f Which is more likely, picking at least one triangle at random or at least one hexagon?

g What is the probability of getting at least one circle?

3 In a Year 9 class 20 students know who Professor Brian Cox is, 16 know who Sir David Attenborough is and 11 know of both. Every student knows of at least one of the men.

a i Write the number who know of both in the section where the circles overlap.

ii How many students need to go in the rest of the Prof. B. circle, so the total in the whole Prof. B. circle is 20? Write this in the diagram.

iii How many students only know of Sir D.? Write this in the diagram.

b How many students are in the Year 9 class? ....

c What is the probability that a student chosen at random knows of both men?

Prof. B.   Sir D.

Mutually exclusive events

4 The table shows the probabilities that Alice is on time, early or late to gym club.

Arrival	on time	early	late
Probability	35%	55%	

What is the probability that Alice is late to gym club? ....

> Alice can't be early and late at the same time, so all the outcomes are _____ _____, so their probabilities add up to _____.
> What percentage must the probabilities of all these outcomes add up to?

Independent events and experimental probability

5 Reasoning / Modelling In an experiment, Hij makes and spins these two spinners 120 times. The table shows his results.

	1	2	3
A	24	21	18
B	23	20	14

Spinner 1   **Spinner 2**

a From these results, estimate the experimental probability of A and 3. ....

b Do you think you could play a fair game with these spinners? Explain your answer.

> Compare the experimental probability to the theoretical probability, as percentages.

c What is the theoretical probability of getting A1? ....

d How many A1 should Hij expect in 120 spins? ....

> Calculate ☐ × 120

6 The tree diagram shows the probabilities of picking milk and plain chocolates from a bag. The first chocolate picked is replaced before the second chocolate is picked.

a Work out the probability of picking two milk chocolates. ....

b Work out the probability of picking

i milk then plain (M, P) ....

ii plain then milk (P, M) ....

iii milk or plain in any order. ....

1st pick   2nd pick

Worked example

> This means (M, P) or (P, M). Do you add or multiply?

9 Extend

1 Problem-solving

Holly spins these two spinners and then adds the scores together.
Is the total more likely to be odd or even? Explain.

Spinner 1   Spinner 2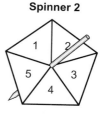

2 Modelling A coin and a dice are used in an experiment.
The coin is flipped and the dice is rolled at the same time.
This is done 600 times. The table shows the results.

	1	2	3	4	5	6
H	49	54	48	52	54	47
T	52	47	48	51	48	50

a Calculate the experimental probability of getting a 5 and a heads from these results.
Give your answer as a percentage.

$$\frac{54}{600} \times 100 = \text{.........................}$$

b Calculate the theoretical probability of getting a 5 and heads.
Give your answer as a percentage.

$$\frac{1}{6} \times \frac{1}{2} \times 100 = \frac{1}{12} \times 100 = \text{.........................}$$

c How many times would you expect to get a 5 and heads from 600 trials? ....

d Do you think that either the coin or the dice was biased? Explain.

'Biased' means 'not fair'.

3 Modelling Box A has 14 chocolates, 4 with nut centres. Box B has 22 chocolates, 8 with nut centres.
Box C has 35 chocolates, 11 with nut centres.

a From which box are you most likely to pick a chocolate with a nut centre? Show your working.

b A chocolate with a nut centre is eaten from box B. Now from which box are you most likely to pick a chocolate with a nut centre?

4 Problem-solving A bag contains strawberry, blackberry, lemon and orange flavoured sweets.
The probability of picking each flavour is given in the table.

Flavour	strawberry	blackberry	lemon	orange
Probability	0.2	0.15	0.25	0.4

a Explain why there must be more than 10 sweets in the bag.

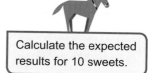

Calculate the expected results for 10 sweets.

b What is the smallest possible number of sweets in the bag?

5 Problem-solving A bag contains red counters and blue counters. Ivan takes out a counter, records its colour and replaces it. He does this 100 times in total. The table shows the results.

Number of trials	25	50	75	100
Number of red counters	8	26	31	43

a Work out the best estimate of the probability of picking a red counter from the bag.

b There are 40 counters in the bag. How many of them are likely to be red?

6 Work out the probability of getting three even numbers when you roll a fair 1–6 dice three times.

>>>>>>
Are the outcomes independent?

7 Reasoning A fair 1–6 dice is rolled twice.
The results are noted as odd or even.

a Draw a tree diagram to show the possible outcomes of rolling a dice twice.

b What is the probability of getting at least
one even number? ....

c What is the probability of getting no
even numbers? ....

d How could you use your answer to part **c** to help you work out the probability of 'at least one even number' more quickly?

8 This tree diagram shows the possible outcomes when a fair coin is flipped three times.

What is the probability of getting heads

a every time ....

b in none of the flips ....

c in only the first and last flips ....

d in at least one of the three flips? ....

1st flip   2nd flip   3rd flip

```
              H —— H
          H
              T —— H
      H           —— T
              H —— H
          T
              T —— H
                 —— T
```

9 a Draw a tree diagram to show the possible outcomes and probabilities of picking a shape from this bag, replacing it, and picking another shape.

b Work out the probability of

   i two squares   **ii** at least one circle.

PROGRESS BAR Colour in the progress bar as you get questions correct. Then fill in the progression chart on pages 104–108.

1 The table shows data about the ages of students in a school canteen.

	13	14	15	16	Total
Males	23	12	8	6	49
Females	15	12	13	11	51
Total	38	24	21	17	100

A student is picked at random. What is the probability that the student is

a a 15-year-old .... **b** a 13-year-old female? ....

One male and one female student are picked at random.

c Which is more likely, that the male will be 14 years old or the female will be 14 years old?

2 a Draw a sample space diagram to show all the possible outcomes of picking one shape from each of these bags.

b What is the probability of picking two of the same shape? ....

3 The Venn diagram shows numbers of parents with 2 children.

a Write the missing words.
  i 19 parents have ....
  ii 11 parents have ....

b One parent is chosen at random.
  What is the probability that they have at least one boy?
  Write your answer as a percentage to the nearest whole number.

4 Aden and Zac spin these fair spinners and add the numbers spun to give a score. What is the probability that the total is

a less than 7 ....
b more than 7 ....
c exactly 7? ....

Aden wins if the score is more than 8, Zac wins if the score is less than 8.

d Is the game fair? Explain your answer.

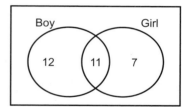

5 Jess kicks two penalties. The probability that she scores a goal is 0.7 for each kick.

a Draw a tree diagram to show the probabilities.

b Work out the probability that she gets exactly one goal.

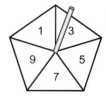

10.1 Congruent and similar shapes

1 Reasoning The diagram shows four congruent isosceles triangles.
Mark equal angles with the same letter. Mark every angle.

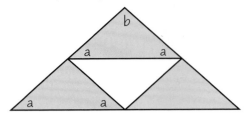

> If all lengths and angles on one shape are equal to the corresponding lengths and angles on another shape, then the shapes are congruent.
> One shape can be a reflection or rotation of the other shape.
> Two shapes are congruent if they are identical.

2 Reasoning For each shape, decide whether it is
congruent to shape A   similar to shape A   neither of these.
Explain how you know.

> Two shapes are similar if one is an enlargement of the other.

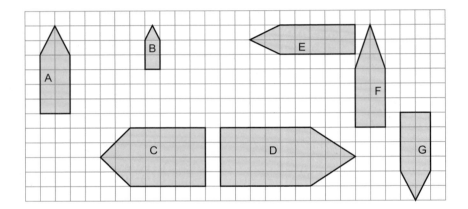

3 Reasoning In this diagram, equal sides and angles are marked.

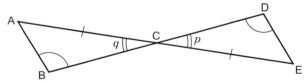

> Triangles are congruent if they have equivalent
> • SSS (all three sides)
> • SAS (two sides and the included angle)
> • ASA (two angles and the included side)
> • AAS (two angles and another side)
> Triangles where all angles are the same (AAA) are similar, but might not be congruent.

a What can you say about angles p and q?

b Show that triangles ABC and EDC are congruent.
   Give the reason for congruency (SSS, SAS, ASA or AAS).

> Draw the two triangles separately to compare them.
>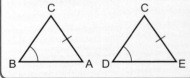

4 Reasoning These triangles are all congruent. Work out the missing sides and angles.

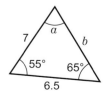 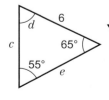

CHECK Tick each box as your **confidence** in this topic improves.

Need extra help? Go to page 99 and tick the boxes next to Q1 and 2. Then have a go at them once you've finished 10.1–10.5.

1 In each part, the three right-angled triangles are similar.
Work out the lengths labelled with letters.

When two shapes are similar, one is an enlargement of the other. This means that pairs of corresponding sides are in the same ratio and their angles are the same (AAA).

a

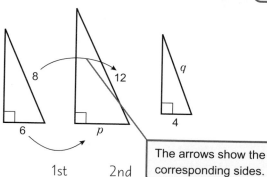

The arrows show the corresponding sides.

b

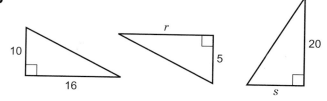

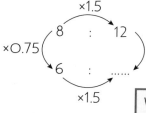

Write down the ratios of corresponding sides.

$p = 6 \times 1.5 = $ ......

2 Are these triangles similar?

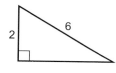 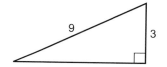

Write down the ratios of corresponding sides.

3 a Show that triangles ABE and ACD are similar.

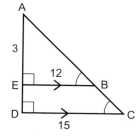

Triangle ABE		Triangle ACD
∠A		∠A
∠E = 90°		∠D = 90°
∠B	=	∠C

The triangles have the same angles (AAA).

Worked example

b Work out length ED.

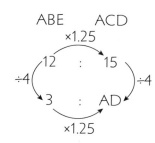

ED = AD – ☐

4 Problem-solving Work out the length labelled a.

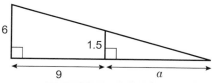

First show that the triangles are similar.

CHECK Tick each box as your **confidence** in this topic improves.

Need extra help? Go to pages 99 and 100 and tick the boxes next to Q3 and 4. Then have a go at them once you've finished 10.1–10.5.

1 On each triangle

   a label the opposite side to angle θ, OPP

   b label the adjacent side to angle θ, ADJ

   c label the hypotenuse side, HYP.

> The Greek letter θ (pronounced theta) is often used for angles.
> The side opposite to the chosen angle (angle θ in this diagram) is called the opposite side.
> The side that runs between the chosen angle and the right angle is called the adjacent side.
> The side opposite to the right angle is called the hypotenuse.
>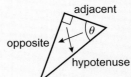

i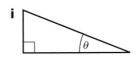

ii

2 Use your calculator to find, correct to 1 decimal place

   a $\tan 8°$ ....

   b $\tan 88°$ ....

> On your calculator enter
>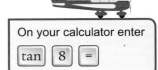

3 Write $\tan \theta$ as $\dfrac{\text{opposite}}{\text{adjacent}}$ for each triangle.

   a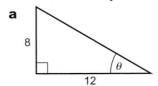

   b

> The ratio of the opposite side to the adjacent side is called the tangent of the angle.
> The tangent of angle θ is written as $\tan \theta$.
> $\tan \theta = \dfrac{\text{opposite}}{\text{adjacent}}$

4 Work out x for each triangle, correct to 1 decimal place.

   a

   b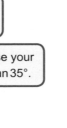

> You can use the tangent ratio to find the length of one of the shorter sides of a right-angled triangle.

Guided

$\tan \theta = \dfrac{\text{opposite}}{\text{adjacent}}$ Write the tangent ratio.

opposite $= x$

adjacent $= 20$ cm   Identify the opposite and adjacent sides.

$\theta = 35°$

$\tan 35° = \dfrac{x}{20}$ Substitute the sides and angle into the tangent ratio.

$20 \times \tan 35° = x$ Multiply both sides by 20. Use your calculator to work out $20 \times \tan 35°$.

$x =$ .... (to 1 d.p.)

5 Real / Modelling A ladder rests against a wall.
The bottom of the ladder is 3 m from the bottom of the wall.
The ladder makes an angle of 55° with the horizontal ground.
How far up the wall does the ladder reach?

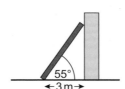

CHECK Tick each box as your **confidence** in this topic improves.

Need extra help? Go to page 100 and tick the boxes next to Q5 and 6. Then have a go at them once you've finished 10.1–10.5.

MASTER # 10.4 The sine ratio

1 Use your calculator to find, correct to 1 decimal place

  a sin 7° ....

  b sin 77° ....

2 Write sin θ as a fraction for each triangle.

a
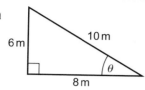

b
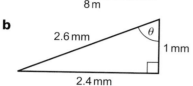

> The ratio of the opposite side to the hypotenuse is called the sine of the angle. The sine of angle θ is written as sin θ.
> $$\sin \theta = \frac{\text{opposite}}{\text{hypotenuse}}$$

3 Work out x for each triangle, correct to 1 decimal place.

a
15 cm, x, 30°

b
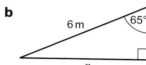
6 m, 65°, x

> You can use the sine ratio to find the length of one of the shorter sides of a right-angled triangle.

Guided

$\sin \theta = \dfrac{\text{opposite}}{\text{hypotenuse}}$ — Write the sine ratio.

opposite = x
hypotenuse = 15 cm — Identify the opposite and hypotenuse sides.

$\theta = 30°$

$\sin 30° = \dfrac{x}{15}$ — Substitute the sides and angle into the sine ratio.

$15 \times \sin 30° = x$ — Multiply both sides by 15.

$x =$ .... (to 1 d.p.)

4 Real / Modelling A 5-metre ladder rests against a wall. The ladder makes an angle of 65° with the horizontal ground. How far up the wall does the ladder reach?

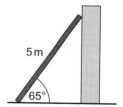
5 m, 65°

5 Modelling A kite flies on the end of a 50 m string. The string makes an angle of 70° to the ground. Use the sine ratio to work out how high the kite is flying. Give your answer to the nearest metre.

Draw a sketch.

CHECK Tick each box as your **confidence** in this topic improves.

Need extra help? Go to page 100 and tick the box next to Q7. Then have a go at it once you've finished 10.1–10.5.

97

10.5 The cosine ratio

 1 Use your calculator to find, correct to 1 decimal place

  a cos 6° ....

  b cos 66° ....

2 Write cos θ as a fraction for each triangle.

  a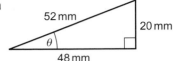

  b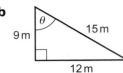

> The ratio of the adjacent side to the hypotenuse is called the cosine of the angle. The cosine of angle θ is written as cos θ.
> $$\cos \theta = \frac{\text{adjacent}}{\text{hypotenuse}}$$

 3 Use the cosine ratio to work out x for each triangle, correct to 1 decimal place.

  a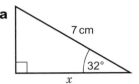

  b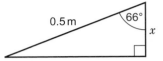

> You can use the cosine ratio to find the unknown lengths of a right-angled triangle.

Guided

$$\cos \theta = \frac{\text{adjacent}}{\text{hypotenuse}}$$ — Write the cos ratio.

adjacent = x — Identify the adjacent and hypotenuse sides.

hypotenuse = 7 cm

θ = 32° — Substitute the sides and angle into the cos ratio.

$$\cos 32° = \frac{x}{7}$$

7 × cos 32° = x — Multiply both sides by 7.

x = ... (to 1 d.p.)

 4 Problem-solving A roof truss is an isosceles triangle, and the sloping side length is 12.5 m. The sloping side makes an angle of 42° to the base of the truss. Use the cosine ratio to find the width of the truss. Give your answer to the nearest centimetre.

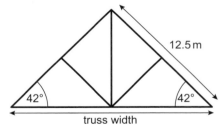

> Divide into two right-angled triangles.
>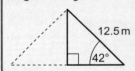

 5 Real The diagram shows the path of a ship that sails 90 km from A. How far south has the ship moved? Give your answer to the nearest kilometre.

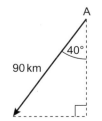

> Use the cosine rule.
>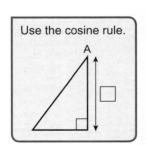

CHECK Tick each box as your **confidence** in this topic improves.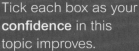

Need extra help? Go to page 100 and tick the box next to Q8. Then have a go at it once you've finished 10.1–10.5.

Congruence and similarity

1 Reasoning Five congruent triangles are arranged like this.
Label all the angles a, b or c so that equal angles have the same letter.

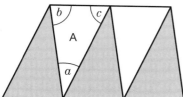

> Trace triangle A. Place it over the other triangles to help you find the equal angles.
> You will need to rotate your tracing for the grey triangles.

2 Three groups of similar shapes have been mixed up.

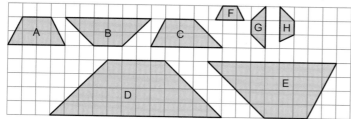

> You could use tracing paper to check whether the angles are the same.

a Look at shapes A and D.

i Are the angles the same?

No, they are different.

ii Are shapes A and D similar?

No.

b Look at shapes B and D.

i Are the angles the same?

Yes.

ii Are shapes B and D similar?

....

c Sort the shapes into three groups of similar shapes.

3 Triangles A and B are similar.

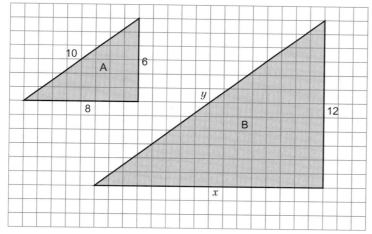

a Complete the table.
Show the pairs of corresponding sides.

b Use a pair of corresponding sides to work out the scale factor from A to B.

6 × .... = 12, so the scale factor is ....

c Use the scale factor to work out x and y.

> A × scale factor = B

Shape	A	B
Height	6	12
Width		x
Hypotenuse	10	

99

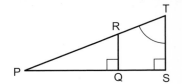

4 Reasoning a What can you say about QR and ST? Explain why.

They are parallel because ....

b Which angle in the diagram is equal to ∠PTS? Explain why.

c Explain why triangles PQR and PST are similar.

d What is the scale factor of the enlargement from triangle PQR to triangle PST?

$48 \times \square = 72$

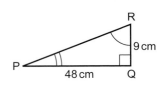

e Work out the length of ST.

$QR \times \square = ST$

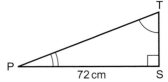

Sine, cosine and tangent

5 On the triangle, label

a 'opp' on the side opposite to ∠θ

b 'adj' on the adjacent side

c 'hyp' on the hypotenuse.

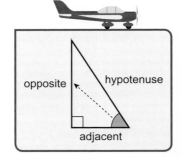

6 Complete to work out the missing length x, correct to 1 decimal place.

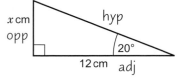

a Write the tangent ratio. tan .... = $\dfrac{\text{...........}}{\text{...........}}$

b Rearrange to make x the subject. x = ... × tan.......

c Use a calculator to find x. ....

Worked example

7 Complete to work out the missing length x, correct to 1 decimal place.

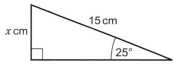

a Write the sine ratio. ....

b Rearrange.   x ....

c Use a calculator to find x. ....

$\sin \theta = \dfrac{\square}{\square}$

8 Complete to work out the missing length x, correct to 1 decimal place.

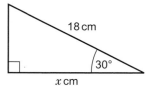

a Write the cos ratio. ....

b Rearrange.   x ....

c Use a calculator to find x. ....

$\cos \theta = \dfrac{\square}{\square}$

1 The line segment AC is split in the ratio $1:4$.

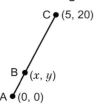

C● (5, 20)

B● (x, y)

A● (0, 0)

a What fraction of AC is AB? ....

b Explain why triangles ABD and ACE are similar.

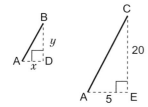

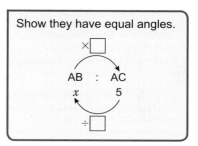

Show they have equal angles.

×☐

AB : AC

x 5

÷☐

c Work out the scale factor. AB × .... = AC

d Use the scale factor to work out x and y.

e Write the coordinates of B. ....

2 The line segment PR is split in the ratio $3:2$.
Work out the coordinates of R.

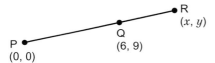

●R
(x, y)

Q
(6, 9)

P ●
(0, 0)

Draw similar triangles, as in Q1.

3 Reasoning The diagram shows two pentagons.
Each has one line of symmetry.

a Show that pentagons ABCDE and PQRST are similar.

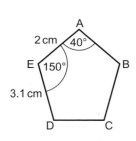

2 cm A 40°

E 150°   B

3.1 cm

D   C

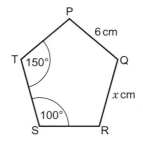

P 6 cm

T 150°   Q

x cm

100°

S   R

b Find the value of x.

4 Real / Problem-solving A flagpole is held in place by four wire ropes.
Each rope is attached to the ground 3.5 metres from the bottom of the flagpole.
The rope makes an angle of 30° with the horizontal ground.
At what height does the rope attach to the flagpole?
Give your answer to the nearest centimetre.

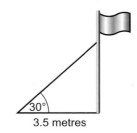

30°
3.5 metres

5 Problem-solving The diagram shows a right-angled triangle in a circle, centre O. The diameter of the circle is 20 cm.
Work out the area of the triangle. Give your answer to 1 decimal place.

Use two ratios, one for the height and one for the base of the triangle.

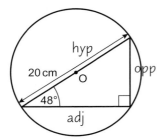

$\sin 48° = \dfrac{opp}{20}$

$opp = 20 × \sin 48°$

$opp =$ ....

$\cos 48° = \dfrac{adj}{20}$

$adj = 20 × \cos 48°$

$adj =$ ....

Area $= \frac{1}{2} ×$ base × height $=$ ....

6 a Complete the following: $\sin 25° = \dfrac{\text{..........}}{\text{..........}}$

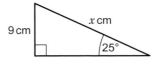

b Rearrange the equation to make x the subject.

c Solve the equation to find the value of x, correct to 1 decimal place.

7 a Label the sides of the triangle 'opposite', 'adjacent' and 'hypotenuse'.

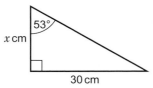

Which ratio uses the two sides labelled 30 cm and x cm?

$\sin \theta = \dfrac{opp}{hyp}$ $\cos \theta = \dfrac{adj}{hyp}$ $\tan \theta = \dfrac{opp}{adj}$

b Which ratio do you need to use to find x, tangent, sine or cosine? ....
c Work out the value of x.

8 a Work out the length BC.

b Work out the length AB.

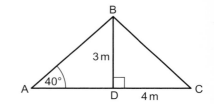

c Work out the length AD.

d Reasoning Is ABC a right-angled triangle? Explain your answer.

9 A zip wire is made from a 200 m length of wire.
The wire is fixed to the top of a 3 m high platform at the top of a cliff.
The wire is fixed to the ground so that its angle to the horizontal is 12°.
How high is the cliff?
Give your answer to the nearest 0.5 m.

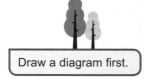

Draw a diagram first.

10 Unit test

1 The diagram shows an arrowhead made from six grey congruent triangles.
Are the white triangles congruent with the grey triangles?
Give reasons for your answer.

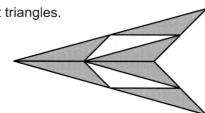

2 Which shapes are similar to shape A? ....

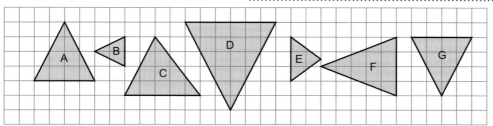

3 These triangles are all congruent. Work out the missing sides and angles.

a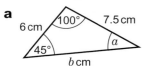

b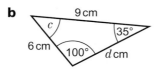

c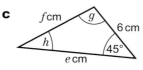

4 Triangles E and F are similar.

   a State the scale factor from E to F. ....

   b Find the value of x. Show your working.

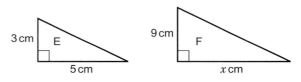

5 The line segment AC is split in the ratio $1:3$.
Work out the coordinates of B.

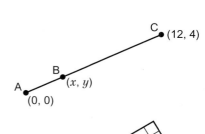

6 Use the tangent ratio to work out the missing length.
Give your answer to 1 d.p.

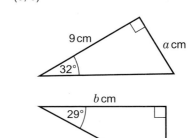

7 Use the cosine ratio to work out the missing length.
Give your answer to 1 d.p.

8 Find the value of x.
Give your answer to 1 d.p.

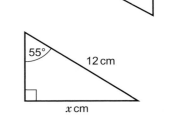

Progression charts

Progression is all about checking your confidence in the maths that you're learning.
- For each Unit test, tick the questions you answered correctly.
- Then rate your confidence by ticking a smiley face.

1 Indices and standard form

I can...	Unit 1: Unit test
Simplify expressions containing powers.	Q3 ☐
Solve word problems using square roots and cube roots	Q2 ☐
Use the prefixes associated with 10^{12}, 10^9, 10^6, 10^3, 10^{-2}, 10^{-3}, 10^{-6}, 10^{-9}, 10^{-12}	Q8 ☐
Know that any number to the power of zero is 1.	Q4 ☐
Make estimates involving more than two operations and BIDMAS.	Q6 ☐ Q7 ☐
Understand the order in which to calculate expressions that contain powers and brackets.	Q5 ☐ Q10 ☐
Apply the index laws for multiplication and division of integer powers.	Q1 ☐
Write and order numbers in standard index form.	Q9 ☐ Q11 ☐ Q12 ☐
My confidence	☹ ☐ 😐 ☐ 🙂 ☐

2 Expressions and formulae

I can...	Unit 2: Unit test
Substitute integers into simple expressions involving small powers.	Q2 ☐ Q5 ☐
Write expressions and formulae.	Q3 ☐
Simplify expressions involving brackets and powers.	Q4 ☐
Apply the index laws including negative power answers.	Q10 ☐
Factorise by taking out an algebraic common factor.	Q6 ☐
Solve equations by substituting.	Q1 ☐
Multiply out brackets and collect like terms.	Q8 ☐
Change the subject of a formula.	Q7 ☐ Q9 ☐
My confidence	☹ ☐ 😐 ☐ 🙂 ☐

3 Dealing with data

I can...	Unit 3: Unit test
Determine suitable sample size and degree of accuracy needed.	Q1 ☐
Discuss factors that may affect the collection of data.	Q2 ☐
Design tables recording discrete and continuous data.	Q3 ☐
Identify key features of data sets, including exceptions and correlation, and use a line of best fit.	Q4 ☐
Find the modal class and calculate an estimate of the mean from a large set of grouped data.	Q5 ☐

My confidence ☹ ☐ 😐 ☐ 🙂 ☐

4 Multiplicative reasoning

I can...	Unit 4: Unit test
Enlarge 2D shapes, given a centre of enlargement and a whole number scale factor.	Q1 ☐
Round numbers to a given number of significant figures.	Q2 ☐
Solve 'original value' problems using inverse operation.	Q3 ☐
Solve problems using compound measures.	Q4 ☐ Q5 ☐
Solve problems using constant rates and related formulae.	Q6 ☐
Calculate percentage change, using the formula $\dfrac{\text{actual change}}{\text{original amount}} \times 100$	Q7 ☐

My confidence ☹ ☐ 😐 ☐ 🙂 ☐

5 Constructions

I can...	Unit 5: Unit test
Use and interpret maps and scale drawings.	Q4 ☐
Use straight edge and compass to construct the mid-point and perpendicular bisector of a line segment.	Q1 ☐
Use straight edge and compass to construct the bisector of an angle.	Q2 ☐
Use straight edge and compass to construct a triangle, given three sides (SSS) or right angle, hypotenuse and side (RHS).	Q5 ☐
Use straight edge and compass to construct perpendiculars.	Q3 ☐
Draw and interpret loci.	Q6 ☐

My confidence ☹ ☐ 😐 ☐ ☺ ☐

6 Equations, inequalities and proportionality

I can...	Unit 6: Unit test		
Know the difference between equations and identities.	Q1 ☐	Q2 ☐	
Convert a recurring decimal to a fraction.	Q7 ☐		
Use algebra to solve problems involving direct proportion.	Q4 ☐	Q8 ☐	
Solve simple linear inequalities and represent the solution on a number line.	Q5 ☐		
Solve simultaneous equations.	Q6 ☐		
Construct and solve equations (including brackets, powers and fractions) with the unknown on both sides.	Q3 ☐		

My confidence ☹ ☐ 😐 ☐ ☺ ☐

7 Circles, Pythagoras and prisms

I can...	Unit 7: Unit test
Solve problems involving the circumference of a circle.	Q1 ☐
Solve problems involving the area of a circle.	Q2 ☐
Find the length of an unknown side of a right-angled triangle	Q3 ☐
Calculate the volumes and surface areas of prisms and cylinders.	Q5 ☐ Q6 ☐
Find upper and lower bounds.	Q4 ☐

My confidence ☹ ☐ 😐 ☐ 🙂 ☐

8 Sequences and graphs

I can...	Unit 8: Unit test
Find the nth term of a sequence.	Q1 ☐
Recognise and continue geometric sequences.	Q2 ☐
Recognise and continue quadratic sequences	Q4 ☐
Interpret graphs.	Q3 ☐ Q6 ☐
Solve simultaneous equations using graphs.	Q7 ☐
Find the equation of a line.	Q8 ☐
Interpret non-linear graphs.	Q5 ☐

My confidence ☹ ☐ 😐 ☐ 🙂 ☐

9 Probability

I can...	Unit 9: Unit test
Calculate and compare probabilities.	Q1 ☐ Q3 ☐
List possible outcomes of one or two events.	Q2 ☐
Calculate the probability of two independent events (including determining whether a game is fair).	Q4 ☐
Use tree diagrams.	Q5 ☐
My confidence ☹ ☐ 😐 ☐ 🙂 ☐	

10 Comparing shapes

I can...	Unit 10: Unit test
Identify similar and congruent shapes.	Q1 ☐ Q2 ☐
Solve problems involving similar and congruent triangles.	Q3 ☐ Q4 ☐ Q5 ☐
Use the tangent ratio to work out the unknown side of a triangle.	Q6 ☐
Use the sine ratio to work out the opposite side in a right-angled triangle.	Q8 ☐
Use the cosine ratio to work out the adjacent side in a right-angled triangle	Q7 ☐
My confidence ☹ ☐ 😐 ☐ 🙂 ☐	